# THE
# SPOOK'S
## APPRENTICE:
## PLAY EDITION

**THE SPOOK'S APPRENTICE: PLAY EDITION**
A RED FOX BOOK 978 1 849 41879 9

*The Spook's Apprentice* first published by the Bodley Head, 2004.

This play edition first published in Great Britain by Red Fox in 2014
Red Fox is an imprint of Random House Children's Publishers UK
A Random House Group Company

1 3 5 7 9 10 8 6 4 2

The Random House Group Limited supports the Forest Stewardship® Council® (FSC®),
the leading international forest-certification organisation. Our books carrying the FSC
label are printed on FSC®-certified paper. FSC is the only forest-certification scheme
supported by the leading environmental organisations, including Greenpeace.
Our paper procurement policy can be found at www.**randomhouse**.co.uk/environment

Set in Minion Pro by Falcon Oast Graphic Art Ltd.

Red Fox Books are published by Random House Children's Publishers UK,
61–63 Uxbridge Road, London W5 5SA

www.**randomhousechildrens**.co.uk
www.**totallyrandombooks**.co.uk
www.**randomhouse**.co.uk

Addresses for companies within The Random House Group Limited
can be found at: www.randomhouse.co.uk/offices.htm

THE RANDOM HOUSE GROUP Limited Reg. No. 954009

A CIP catalogue record for this book is available from the British Library.

Printed and bound in Great Britain by Clays Ltd, St Ives plc

# JOSEPH DELANEY
## ~THE~
# SPOOK'S
## APPRENTICE:
## PLAY EDITION

**ADAPTED BY STEPHEN DELANEY**

**ILLUSTRATIONS BY DAVID WYATT**

RED FOX

JOSEPH DELANEY

— THE —

SPOOK'S

A PPRENTICE:
PLAY EDITION

ADAPTED BY STEPHEN DELANEY

*With special thanks to*
RUSSELL WOODHEAD

# CHARACTERS

THE SPOOK .................. Tom's new master; protects the County against the dark

DAD ................................. Tom's father, a farmer

TOM WARD .................. The Spook's new apprentice

SNOUT ............................ A slaughterman

JACK ................................ Tom's elder brother

ELLIE ............................. His wife

MAM ............................... Tom's mother

ANDREW ....................... The Spook's brother, a locksmith

PRIEST

GHAST

THREE BOYS

ALICE .............................. A young witch

VILLAGERS:
GROCER
BAKER
BUTCHER
SEAMSTRESS
TEACHER
MIDWIFE

MESSENGER
MOTHER MALKIN ..... A witch
BONY LIZZIE ................ A witch
TUSK ............................... An abhuman
TOMMY .......................... A young boy

# ACT ONE

# SCENE ONE
## OUTSIDE THE WARD FAMILY FARM

*Stage left, the front door and windows of the house; stage right,
the fence separating the house from a lane. A path comes
round the corner of the house and towards the gate.
Downstage there is a low, wide tree stump. Upstage, we can
see some small hedges and, in the distance, Hangman's Hill.*

*THE SPOOK, DAD and TOM are standing in the
front garden of the house.*

THE SPOOK: You're sure he's the seventh?

DAD: Aye, that he is.

THE SPOOK: And you were a seventh son too?

DAD: Aye, just like I told you. The eldest of my
boys got the farm, and I've found trades for
the other five. That just leaves Tom here –
number seven.

THE SPOOK: How old is he?

DAD: Thirteen come August.

THE SPOOK: Bit small for his age.

DAD: Aye, but he's strong. His six brothers have
given him plenty of practice at fighting. And
when he grows up, he'll be as big as me!

1

**THE SPOOK:**   That may be, but mine is a hard enough life for a man, never mind a boy. Can he read and write?

**DAD:**   He can do both, and he knows Greek – spoke it before he could walk. His mam taught him.

**THE SPOOK** (*turning to Tom*):
  How do you like school, lad? Enjoy your studies?

**TOM:**   They hit me, sir. I don't go any more.

**THE SPOOK:**   And why would they do that?

**TOM:**   I write with my left hand. When the teachers saw that, they tied the pen to my right one and tried to beat it out of me. That's when Mam brought me home to teach me herself.

**THE SPOOK** (*raising his staff in his left hand*):
  Nothing wrong with being cack-handed, Tom. A boggart doesn't mind which hand it's caught with.

**DAD:**   How much to take him on?

**THE SPOOK:**   Two guineas for a month's trial. If he's up to it, I'll be back again in the autumn, and you'll owe me another ten. If not, you can have him back and it's just one more guinea for my trouble.

**DAD** (*fishing a pouch of coins out of his pocket*):
>>> Seems a bit much to me, for a job that won't gain him any friends. If I hadn't run out of favours to call in—

**THE SPOOK:** Seventh sons of seventh sons are easier to find than you'd think. If you'd rather I found another one . . .

**DAD** (*eagerly pressing the purse into the Spook's palm*):
>>> No no, Mr Gregory, let's not be hasty. And besides, it's what the boy's mam wants for him.

*DAD wipes the hand that touched THE SPOOK on a trouser leg.*

**THE SPOOK:** I've some business close by but I'll be back for the lad at first light. Make sure he's ready. I don't like to be kept waiting.

*The SPOOK exits.*

*Noise of a horse and cart from behind the house.*

**DAD:** That'll be Snout, coming to look at the pigs we've been fattening . . . Listen, son, before I go and talk to him, I've got something for you.

**TOM:** What is it, Dad?

**DAD:**  I've never had a lot to give you, Tom, and you would never have had a farm to grow up on if it wasn't for your mother's money. But part of me wishes you weren't going. You'll be missed, that's for sure.

*DAD takes a tinderbox from his pocket and gives it to TOM.*

**DAD:**  It's my old tinderbox, from when I was a lad. You might find it useful one day, if you're in need of a fire, and every time you hold it I want you to think of how proud I am of you.

**TOM:**  I will, Dad. Thanks.

**DAD:**  There are many things you will discover on your journey, but you must always remember you're ours. It's a new life for you now, son . . .

*DAD trails off, overcome by emotion. He tries to conceal it by coughing.*

**DAD:**  Dear me, I think I've got something in my throat. You go and get yourself cleaned up. You're finished with farming now!

*SNOUT enters, wearing an apron covered in blood stains.*

**DAD:**  Snout! I hope you're feeling generous – I'm looking for a good deal today.

SNOUT:   You all right, Mr Ward?

DAD:   Fine, Snout.

SNOUT:   So, Master Tom! I presume the appearance of old man Gregory means yer time has come. Off to get the ghosties, eh?!

*SNOUT staggers towards TOM like a monster. TOM steps back, annoyed.*

DAD:   Leave him alone, Snout! My boy'll do well.

SNOUT:   Good luck, lad. You'll need it from what I hear. Now, I hope you've been feeding them pigs properly, Mr Ward. Last lot didn't have enough meat on them for a bacon sandwich . . .

*The conversation fades as DAD and SNOUT exit.*

*TOM is left alone onstage. He smiles and looks at the tinderbox.*

*Just as TOM turns to leave in the opposite direction, he is surprised by JACK and ELLIE, appearing from behind a bush. ELLIE is pregnant and has a small bump.*

JACK:   I don't believe it!

*Laughing, JACK gets TOM in a playful headlock.*

5

JACK:      You, apprentice to a spook! How can *you* do a job like that when you still can't sleep without a candle?

ELLIE:      Let him go!

*JACK does so.*

ELLIE:      Well done, Tom. I'm really pleased for you.

JACK:      Me too. You'll make a fortune doing that job. And that's lucky . . .

TOM:      Why's that?

JACK:      Because the only friends you'll have are the ones you buy!

ELLIE:      Oh, Jack! Don't be cruel!

TOM:      He's given me a month's trial. Maybe I won't be any good at it.

ELLIE:      Oh no, Tom! That means you won't be here when the baby's born.

TOM:      I'll come back and visit as soon as I can.

ELLIE:      You'll always have your family right here if you need us.

JACK:             Just leave the ghosts on Hangman's Hill!

*MAM enters.*

MAM:              Is your brother giving you trouble, Tom?

JACK:             Just teasing, Mam.

MAM:              Why don't you go and give your father a
                  hand with the pigs, Jack.

JACK (*reluctantly*):
                  If someone's got to do it . . .

MAM:              It may as well be you, yes. Ellie, there's some
                  potatoes need peeling in the kitchen.

ELLIE:            Don't leave without saying goodbye, Tom!

*JACK and ELLIE exit.*

MAM:              Come and sit with me, Tom.

*MAM sits down on a tree stump. TOM sits cross-legged at her feet.*

MAM:              Well, Tom. It's a big step leaving home and
                  starting out on your own, and this is the last
                  time we'll get to talk together for quite a
                  while. If there's anything you need to say,
                  anything you need to ask, now's the time to
                  do it.

*An awkward silence. TOM stares at the ground and fiddles with the tinderbox.*

MAM:  What's wrong? Cat got your tongue? Stop fidgeting, Tom, and concentrate. How do you feel about starting your new job?

TOM:  Mam, nobody wants to go anywhere near a spook. I'll have no friends, I'll be lonely all the time, and . . . and . . .

MAM:  It won't be as bad as you think. You'll have your master to talk to. Mr Gregory will be your teacher, and I expect he'll eventually become your friend too. For nearly sixty years he's walked the borders of the County doing his duty. Doing what has to be done. And although he's strong now, his time will soon come to an end. Then it'll be your turn. And if you won't do it, who will? Who'll look after the ordinary folk? Who'll keep them from harm? Who'll make the farms, villages and towns safe so that women and children can walk the streets and lanes free from fear? Besides, you'll be busy all the time. Busy learning new things. You'll have no time to feel lonely. Don't you think that's exciting?

TOM:  It's exciting but it's scary. I want to go, although I don't know if I can do it. I want to travel and see interesting places, but it'll be hard not living here any more. I'll miss you all. I'll be homesick.

MAM (*her tone sharpening*):

You can't stay here. Your dad's getting too old to work, and come next winter he's handing the farm over to Jack. Ellie will be having her baby soon, no doubt the first of many; eventually there won't be room for you here. You'd better get used to it before that happens. You can't come back home. You're not only going to do this job, you're going to do it well. I bore six sons so that I could have you. Seven times seven you are, and you have the gift that brings, whether it's a curse or a blessing.

TOM:

But didn't you *want* to have the others?

MAM:

Of course, I love every one of them. But in the whole wide County you're the only person who's really like me. You're special. You might feel like a boy who's still a lot of growing to do, but you've the gift and the strength to do what has to be done. I know you're going to make me proud of you.

*Pause.*

TOM:

I think I understand, Mam.

*MAM turns to face upstage.*

MAM:          What do you hear coming from Hangman's Hill?

TOM (*nervously*): I can hear the branches creaking, Mam. Dead soldiers are hanging there. I can hear them swinging and choking.

MAM:          But is there anything *really* hanging from those branches?

TOM:          No.

MAM:          That's right. I hear those noises as well. Like you, I sense those dead soldiers from years ago. Your brothers don't. And why is that? We have gifts others don't. Now, go and pack your bag before dinner. It's a big day tomorrow and you need to get an early night and be at your best. Be sure to take writing paper, won't you?

*TOM gets up from the ground.*

TOM:          I will, and I promise I'll write. Thanks, Mam. Goodnight.

*TOM gives MAM a kiss on the cheek and goes into the house.*

*MAM is left staring out at Hangman's Hill.*

MAM:          Good luck, Thomas Ward. I hope I've done the right thing.

# SCENE TWO
## NUMBER 13, WATERY LANE

*The front of the Ward farmhouse has been changed to the inside wall of 13 Watery Lane. The room is bare, just a flagged floor and a heap of dirty straw under the windows, which are hung with tattered, yellowing lace curtains. A single candle already burns inside the house, sitting on a tiny low table, and some light enters through the curtains. Another closed door stands stage right. An empty stage. We hear voices approaching the house, and a clock striking seven in the distance.*

ANDREW (*offstage*):

You don't give your apprentices much of a break, John. How long have you had him carrying that bag?

THE SPOOK (*offstage*):

I'm a spook and you're a locksmith, brother! Keep your opinions to yourself. The boy's got to get used to hardship if he's going to take over from me. Is the house secure?

ANDREW (*offstage*):

As ordered, John. The lock's a solid one: no one's been in.

*A jangling of keys in the lock. The door swings open.*

*Enter the SPOOK, first, followed by ANDREW, and TOM, carrying a heavy bag.*

**THE SPOOK:** Here we are, lad. Number thirteen Watery Lane. I bring all my new apprentices here so I can find out what they're made of. Are you sure you're ready? It's not too late to change your mind, get yourself a nice safe trade. How about chimney sweep?

**TOM:** No, I'm ready.

**ANDREW:** So you're Tom Ward?

**TOM:** Yes, sir.

**ANDREW:** Bought a cow off your father a while back. Honest man, he is. I'm Andrew – your master's brother.

*TOM swings the bag off his shoulder and dumps it down to shake hands with ANDREW.*

*PRIEST enters through the open front door.*

**ANDREW:** Good evening, Matthew.

**THE SPOOK** (*abruptly*):
What's *he* doing here?

**ANDREW:** I asked him to join us. We're family. I know you're not of the faith, but the lad will need all the help he can get.

PRIEST:        Please, John, permit me to do one thing. We share the same blood.

*THE SPOOK sighs and nods reluctantly.*

*PRIEST goes over to TOM and makes the sign of the cross on him.*

PRIEST:        In the name of the Father, the Son and the Holy Ghost. Are you prepared for what's behind that door, boy?

TOM:        Yes. (*To Spook*) Yes, I am!

PRIEST:        You have the Lord's protection . . . John, are you sure about this?

THE SPOOK (*irritated*):

        He'll be fine! Now out! Both of you! Let's leave the lad to it.

*ANDREW and PRIEST exit.*

THE SPOOK:        Your mother has spoken to you, hasn't she? Told you that you *have* to be a spook's apprentice?

TOM:        Yes, sir. How did you know?

THE SPOOK:        The look on your face tells me you're reluctant to do this. But you're on your own now, if you ignore the rats in the corner, so it's your choice whether you stay or not. I've got business to attend to, but I'll be back to pick you up.

TOM: What do I do?

THE SPOOK: At the stroke of midnight you're to go down into the cellar and face whatever it is that's lurking there. Cope with that and you're well on your way to being taken on permanently. Any questions?

TOM: No, sir.

THE SPOOK: How will you know when it's midnight?

TOM: It's just gone seven now. I'll listen for twelve chimes from the church clock.

THE SPOOK: Good lad. When the clock strikes twelve, take the stub of the candle there and find your way down to the cellar. Until then, sleep – if you can manage it. Now listen carefully – there are three important things to remember. Don't open the front door to anyone, no matter how hard they knock, and don't be late going down to the cellar.

*THE SPOOK walks to the front door.*

**TOM:**        What's the third thing?

**THE SPOOK:**        The candle, lad. Whatever you do, don't let it go out!

*THE SPOOK exits.*

*TOM walks to the cellar door and tries the handle, but it's stuck. He struggles for a moment before returning to the pile of straw and sitting down.*

*The last of the light from the windows quickly fades, so that TOM sits in a pool of light next to the candle.*

**TOM:**        Well, no use just sitting here waiting . . . I'll write to Mam.

*He pulls out a pen and paper from his bag and begins to write a letter.*

*The church clock strikes eight times. TOM writes for a moment longer, then puts away the pen and paper. He pulls off a boot and takes a brush from his bag. He begins to scrub at the mud on his boot.*

*The church clock strike nine times. TOM yawns and pulls his boots back on. As he does so, we hear the single strike of a shovel hitting dirt.*

*TOM raises his head to listen, but there is no further noise. Just as he returns to tying up his boot laces, the sound comes again.*

*TOM hastily tucks his laces in and presses his back to the wall. The shovel strikes again, then becomes rhythmic. TOM pulls his bag to him, hiding his face.*

*The digging stops suddenly and the shovel clatters to the floor. We hear the sound of heavy boots climbing the stone steps from the cellar. A loud sound of breathing.*

**TOM** (*trembling*):

> Who's there ...? I said, *Who's there?* I can hear you breathing! I'm not afraid of you!

*A large dark silhouette enters stage right and stands behind the closed door. The figure tries the handle, shaking the door vigorously.*

**TOM:**  Go away! You're not real and you can't hurt me! (*Shouting*) I SAID, LEAVE ME ALONE!

*Suddenly the figure turns and exits and the noise ceases. TOM is left in silence. After a few moments, the clock strikes ten.*

**TOM:**  If that was the worst that's going to happen tonight, I think I'll get through it! Now I just wait until midnight, go down to the cellar, and get out of here.

*There are three loud raps on the front door, near TOM's head. TOM turns and retreats from the door, into the darkness in the centre of the room.*

TOM: I spoke too soon!

MAM'S VOICE (*offstage*):
Tom! Tom! Open the door! Let me in!

TOM (*standing and rushing to the door*):
Mam, Mam, I'm coming!

MAM'S VOICE (*offstage*):
Quickly, Tom, quickly! Don't keep me
waiting!

*TOM starts to lift the latch, then pauses.*

TOM: But Mr Gregory told me never to let anyone
in, Mam. If I open the door, I fail his test.

MAM'S VOICE (*offstage*):
Never mind, Tom! Let me in!

TOM (*backing away from the door*):
Hang on, how did you know I was here? Why
isn't Dad or Jack with you at this hour? This
isn't right. Who are you?

*The knocking gets louder.*

MAM'S VOICE (*crying*):
Please let me in, Tom! How can you be so
hard and cruel? I'm wet through and I'm
freezing.

TOM:             I don't know who you are, but you're not my
                 mother. Mam would never cry!

*There is a scream and a final pound on the door, then silence
returns.*

*TOM returns to the pile of straw and sits down. It is raining
outside. The clock chimes eleven times. With the final chime, the
rhythmic sound of digging comes from the cellar again, louder
than before. Again the footsteps start to climb the staircase and we
hear breathing.*

TOM:             It's no use – I'm not afraid any more! The
                 door's locked and you can't come in! I'm not
                 scared of ghosts or spirits or whatever you
                 are, so why don't you just—

*The figure appears behind the door and immediately throws it
open with a crash of thunder.*

*THE GHAST slowly walks towards TOM.*

TOM:             No! You can't take me!

*THE GHAST reaches tom, picks him up and begins dragging him
by the scruff of the neck towards the cellar door.*

TOM (*screaming*): Help! Help! Mr Gregory, where are you?
                 Please, put me down, whoever you are.
                 (*Choking*) I can't breathe. Please don't bury
                 me!

*TOM makes a desperate grab for the candle and knocks it to the floor, extinguishing it.*

**TOM:**   No, the candle! The rules! Please stop, I don't deserve this, I've done nothing – nothing to you! Let me go, I beg you! Please let me *go*!

*TOM wrenches himself free and dashes for the candle, pulling the tinderbox from his pocket. He quickly relights the candle, and in a burst of light from the tinderbox and lightning through the windows, THE GHAST disappears.*

*The thunder and lightning subside and the rain continues quietly. TOM turns to the cellar door and finds the room empty. He goes to the door and shuts it, then picks up his bag and heads for the front door to leave. He pauses by the door.*

**TOM:**   No, I can't run out now. I have to do it. I can't let Mam down.

*TOM puts the bag down and sits on the straw. He relaxes against the wall and yawns, then slowly curls up on the floor and goes to sleep.*

*The rain gradually becomes quieter until there is total silence. Twelve chimes of the church clock wake TOM.*

**TOM** (*whispering*):
          It's time.

*TOM picks up the candle stub and makes his way to the cellar door. He opens it and steps into the darkness beyond. As he does so, we can hear his heart beating quickly.*

# SCENE THREE
## THE CELLAR

*In the momentary blackout, the hay, table, bag and door have been removed, and a collection of barrels have appeared downstage-left. There are cobwebs and dust everywhere.*

*We continue to hear TOM's heartbeat. Enter tom, straining his eyes. His candle seems to light the room dimly. There is a musty smell that makes him cover his nose. He pauses as he hears something from behind the barrels. Taking a deep breath, TOM walks towards the barrels, his heartbeat becoming deafeningly loud. Just as he arrives, a dark figure rises suddenly from behind the casks.*

**THE SPOOK:**    What kept you? You're nearly five minutes late!

*TOM slumps to the floor in relief, breathing heavily. His heartbeat ceases and there is silence again.*

**THE SPOOK:**    Nothing to say? You've done well, lad. You've undergone an ordeal, but you've come through it!

*TOM continues to stare at the floor.*

**THE SPOOK:**    Hmm, taken the wind out of you, has it? It did me too. I expect you're wondering why I brought you here and put you through this. Well, I lived in this house as a child, and I saw and heard things that would make your toes curl. But I was the only one who could, and

21

so my dad used to beat me for telling lies.
Something used to climb out of the cellar
and haunt me. It would have been the same
for you. Am I right?

*TOM nods.*

**THE SPOOK:**    Well, terrifying as it was, it's nothing to worry
about, lad. It's just a ghast. That's a fragment
of a troubled soul that's now gone on to
better things. He had to leave the bad part of
himself behind or he'd have been stuck here
for ever.

**TOM:**    What did he do? Why's he got a bad part?

*THE SPOOK takes a seat on a barrel.*

**THE SPOOK:**    He was a miner whose lungs were so diseased
that he couldn't work any more. He spent his
days and nights coughing and struggling for
breath while his wife had to work in the
bakery to keep them both. There aren't very
many women in the world you can trust, lad,
and the pretty ones are worst of all – that's
something you should know by now. Such a
pretty one, thought the miner, was his wife.
To make it worse, the miner was a jealous
man and his illness made him bitter. He was
torn up with questioning whether his wife
was faithful to him.

*Heavy breathing fills the room.*

GHAST:         She was beautiful. And I was right. Too
                   right!

*TOM gasps. THE GHAST is just visible in the gloom, stage right.*

THE SPOOK:     You hear his voice, just as I did! All these
                   years he's refused to accept the truth. Tom,
                   this is your chance, your first chance to
                   communicate with the dark. Ask it a
                   question! Come on, lad, don't be afraid!

*TOM stands up to address THE GHAST.*

TOM:            Er . . . Why are you still here?

GHAST (*struggling for breath*):
                   Everything taken from me. Worked hard,
                   every day. Long days. Got me lungs bad.
                   Couldn't work no more.

THE SPOOK (*standing*):
                   Cut to it, ghast!

GHAST:         I waited for her. But she didn't come home.
                   Two hours late.

THE SPOOK:     No reason to do what you did!

GHAST:         Wrenched my heart. Certain she was with a

man. Heard them laugh on the street corner. Sure of it. Sure I did!

THE SPOOK: By the time his wife arrived, any goodness in him had been wrung out like dirty water from a dish cloth. He waited behind the front door in such a rage that he broke his pretty wife's head open with a big cob of coal as she came through it. And then he left her there, dying on the flags, and went down to the cellar to dig a grave. She was still alive when he came back, but she couldn't move or cry out. That's the terror that comes to us. It's how she felt as he picked her up and carried her down into the darkness. She knew what was happening, but she didn't know why.

TOM: I could feel all that.

THE SPOOK: That's because it's the truth, and now the only thing left is his ghast before you, the dark fragment of himself, left here to suffer.

GHAST: I took my own life.

*THE GHAST exits.*

THE SPOOK: The ghast's memory and guilt is strong enough to torment folks like us because we see things others don't. We live with a blessing and a curse, boy. But it's a very useful thing in our trade.

TOM: How could you live here, Mr Gregory?

THE SPOOK: One night I was so terrified that I screamed out and woke the whole house up, and in a rage my father carried me down into the cellar. He got a hammer and nailed the door shut with me behind it. I was seven at the most. I climbed back up the steps and scratched and banged at the door, fit to burst. But my father was a hard man and I knew I'd be there until long after dawn. After I'd calmed down, do you know what I did?

*TOM shakes his head.*

THE SPOOK: I walked down the steps and sat in the darkness. I took three deep breaths and faced my fear – faced the darkness, which is the most terrifying thing of all for people like us. Things come to us in the dark. They seek us out with whispers and take shapes only *our* eyes can see. But face the dark I did, and when I left this cellar, I knew: there is nothing in this house that can harm you – as long as you're brave. The dark feeds on fear. Remember that well.

*THE SPOOK blows out the candle and there is complete darkness.*

**THE SPOOK:**    This is it, lad. Just you, me and the dark. Can you stand it? Are you fit to be my apprentice?

**TOM:**    Someone has to do it, so it might as well be me.

**THE SPOOK** (*bursting into laughter*):
    You have a lot to learn, but you'll do!

*TOM nervously laughs with THE SPOOK.*

# SCENE FOUR
## THE LANE

*Three boys of TOM's age are hanging about at
the side of the road.*

BOY 1:        Oi, Matty, why weren't you in school today?

BOY 2:        Had to help Dad getting the field planted,
didn't I? Dad reckons it's work first, school
second this time of year, 'specially after last
year's harvest.

BOY 3:        You're lucky. Missed that stupid test.

BOY 1:        No point – he'd've got about none right
anyway.

BOY 2:        Shut up, Arthur. Least I don't wet myself
when Sir gets out the Latin books.

BOY 1 (*launching himself at Boy 2*):
        Hey, that never happened!

BOY 2:        Oi, get off me! I'll tell y' dad!

*The two boys are tussling on the ground. BOY 3 goes to separate
them, then spots something offstage.*

BOY 3:        Hey! Stop it! Look who it is!

*The others look, then quickly separate themselves and stand up, forming a line blocking the road.*

*TOM enters slowly, carrying a large sack over his shoulder.*

**BOY 1** (*intimidatingly*):
'Ello, Lefty! Thought we'd never see you again.

**TOM:** Hello, Arthur. Hi, boys.

**BOY 1:** What's in the sack?

**TOM:** Nothing. I mean, just the week's provisions for my master.

**BOY 1:** Open it up and let's see what you've got.

**TOM** (*gripping the sack tightly*):
I'm sorry, but whatever's in it is my master's first and mine second. I'll be in trouble if it doesn't get home safe and sound.

**BOY 2:** Your master?

**TOM:** Yes. This doesn't belong to me, it belongs to Mr Gregory. The Spook.

**BOY 3:** Yeah, we know who he is. Mr Gregory's last apprentice always gave us a little morsel, didn't he, boys? Where's ya generosity, Lefty?

*BOY 3 has moved downstage to distract TOM from BOY 2, who is sneaking up behind him.*

**BOY 1:**   Don't use big words, Will – he doesn't go to school.

**TOM:**   I'm learning things you can't learn in school.

**BOY 3:**   Like being a dogsbody?

**BOY 1:**   We can do this the easy way, or the hard way, but you won't like the hard way much.

**TOM:**   Well, I'm not giving you the bag.

**BOY 2:**   Fine by us.

*BOY 2 grabs tom from behind, snatching the sack. BOY 1 and BOY 3 descend on tom, forcing him to the ground. The boys take TOM's sack to centre stage and open it.*

**BOY 2** (*pulling out an apple*):
   I'm hungry – I'm having this.

**BOY 3** (*pulling out bread*):
   Me 'n' all.

**BOY 1** (*laughing*):
   Spook's last apprentice didn't get any bruises! Not from us, anyway . . .

*ALICE has entered upstage. She is wearing a black dress, tied tightly at the waist with a piece of white string, and long, pointy shoes.*

**ALICE:** Why don't you give that back?

*Everyone stops and looks at ALICE.*

**BOY 1** (*menacingly*):
What's it to you?

**ALICE:** Ain't me you need to worry about. Lizzie's back, and if you don't do what I say, I'll just tell her you've annoyed me, and then it's her you'll answer to.

**TOM:** Lizzie?

**ALICE:** Bony Lizzie. She's my aunt. These boys can tell you all about her.

*The boys have stood up and are backing away from ALICE.*

**ALICE:** Go on! Be off with you! Be quick or be dead!

*The boys turn and exit, running.*

**ALICE:** Ain't you going to run as well?

*TOM shakes his head, and says nothing. He goes to the sack and starts putting the food back in.*

**ALICE** (*going to help him*):

Don't worry, we can be friends. Ain't nothing
to worry about really – I just said them
things to scare off those boys. People don't
like Bony Lizzie round here, but I'm her
favourite niece, and I'm not frightening,
am I?

**TOM:** I suppose not.

**ALICE:** Well, don't look so down in the mouth then.
'Ere, ain't you going to thank me? Be nice to
get some thanks.

**TOM** (*standing up*):

I'm sorry, you're right, I'm being very rude.
Thank you very much for your help.

**ALICE:** You're welcome. I'm Alice.

**TOM:** It's very nice to meet you, Alice. I'm Tom.

*They shake hands. TOM takes a cake from the sack.*

**TOM:** Here, take this. I suppose since I eat my
master's food, at least one of these is mine to
give – I just won't have one later.

**ALICE:** No thanks, I'm not hungry.

**TOM:** Oh.

ALICE: But if you really want to thank me, there is one thing you could do . . . I mean, only if you wanted to.

TOM: What's that?

ALICE: Ain't going to tell you now. Tell you tomorrow night, I will, just as the sun goes down. Come to me when you hear Old Gregory's bell.

TOM: Old Gregory? You mean *Mr* Gregory. Not many people dare refer to my master like that.

ALICE: Ain't many people like me. Come when you hear the bell. But come alone!

*ALICE starts heading back towards the village. TOM picks up the sack and swings it over his shoulder*

ALICE (*stopping*): Oh, and, Tom – take care now. You don't want to end up like Old Gregory's last apprentice.

TOM: What happened to him?

ALICE: Better ask your master.

*ALICE exits. tom stands there for a moment, then continues across the stage and exits.*

# SCENE FIVE
## THE SPOOK'S GARDEN

*TOM and THE SPOOK are sitting by a tree, the spook making notes in a large leather-bound volume. TOM is holding a small notebook. A large bell hangs from a tree in the distance.*

TOM:            What's this?

THE SPOOK:      Sixty sheets of blank white paper.

TOM:            What's it for?

THE SPOOK:      This, lad, is the most important thing I will ever give you. It is *now* a blank notebook but it will *become* your bestiary, your encyclopaedia. In this you will record every single foe we encounter. There will be written descriptions, detailed drawings, maps, spells and, most importantly, notes on your experiences. From these you will learn the most!

TOM:            And when will we encounter these 'foes'? I've been your apprentice for nearly two weeks, and all I've done is fetch you food from the village. I think all the witches must be on holiday.

THE SPOOK:      Witches are never far away, Tom, and they certainly don't go on *holiday*.

**TOM:**          I wouldn't know. I've never seen one.

*THE SPOOK sighs.*

**THE SPOOK:**          Maybe you're right, lad. Maybe you are ready
to start your training.

*He stands up.*

**THE SPOOK:**          Come on, then.

**TOM:**          Where are we going?

**THE SPOOK:**          To the eastern garden.

*THE SPOOK leads TOM in a circle around the stage as it
gradually darkens.*

**THE SPOOK:**          It's safe enough when the sun's up, but never
walk down this path after dark. Well, not
unless you have a very good reason – and
certainly not when you're alone.

**TOM:**          It's cold down here.

*They stop at the edge of the stage, as if looking into a pit.*

**THE SPOOK:**          Look down there, lad. What do you see?

*TOM bends down cautiously.*

TOM (*stepping back in shock*):
        Feet! It's a body hung upside down.

THE SPOOK:    Can you make out the shape of the feet?

TOM:    They're round at the back and pointy at the front. And they're shoes, not feet.

THE SPOOK:    Exactly right. Lesson one, lad, always look closer! Pointy shoes – that's the calling sign of the witch. It's traditional, and a warning to others to stay away. No fool would wear pointy shoes in these parts unless she was a witch! Note that down and underline it! Those feet down there belong to Mother Malkin – bad news even by witch standards!

TOM (*his gaze fixed on the pit*):
        Yes, sir.

THE SPOOK:    Some witches will hide their pointy shoes when they see us – we're their worst nightmare! – so if you get a chance to see the actual foot, watch out for the same pointy shape. An old witch will have pressed her toes into those vile shoes for so long, they look like the point of a pickaxe. Truth be told, lad, all women are trouble – pointy shoes or no.

TOM:    That's not true! My mam's a woman.

THE SPOOK:     So she is! And done a good job of raising you,
               she has! But she is, shall we say, a complicated
               woman. Right, tell me about the barrels you
               noticed by the kitchen door.

TOM:           Salt, sir. Salt and iron filings, I think.

THE SPOOK:     Impressive powers of observation! Salt and
               iron filings. Use them well and a witch's
               powers can be greatly reduced. Give you a
               chance to bind them with this . . .

*THE SPOOK pulls a length of thin chain from his pocket.*

TOM:           But that wouldn't bind a lamb, Mr Gregory!

THE SPOOK:     It's not just any old chain, Tom, it's silver –
               one of our most important weapons.

*TOM looks nervous. He scribbles in his notebook.*

THE SPOOK:     Once you've bound a witch with a chain, you
               can put her in one of these. (*Gestures to the
               pit at their feet*) The other options are
               burning her, or eating her heart, but I don't
               hold with that sort of thing myself.

TOM:           How much salt and iron do I use?

THE SPOOK:     It's not how much, but how accurate your
               throw is – just like the chain. I'll give you

training, and plenty of it, don't worry!
There'll be times when you think your arm's
going to drop off, but repetition is the only
way to crack it.

TOM: I was always good at throwing.

THE SPOOK: Of course, it's easy if you can *see* the witch.
Possession's another matter . . .

TOM (*scribbling*): But you said the feet were a giveaway.

THE SPOOK: That only applies to a witch in her own body.
Destroy a witch's own flesh and she'll look
for another host. Then it's about reading the
signs. A newly possessed body will be
unsteady on its feet. Like a new pair of shoes,
it takes a while for the witch to get used to
her new body. That, and the temper on them!
A witch will do anything to hold onto a new
body once she's found one.

TOM: I can't keep up!

THE SPOOK: There's a book in my library that will help.
But for now, the sun's going down and my
stomach is rumbling. Can you smell our
food, lad?

TOM: Yes, sir. But . . . who's preparing our dinner?
You've been here with me the whole time.

THE SPOOK: Happy to see you making use of rule two:
never be afraid to ask! Our cook for the
evening is a boggart. A boggart is a type of
spirit, as you know, but this particular one
is . . . Well, I'll teach you so much about
boggarts, they will be coming out of yer ears!
For tonight, all you need to know is that this
one guards the house and carries out
domestic duties, and in return it gets . . . this
garden. Anything that's not welcome in this
garden . . . the boggart can have its blood. It
will keep you safe when I'm away.

TOM: I hope you told it that *I'm* welcome.

THE SPOOK: I think you'd better come in and meet it –
let's go and wash our hands. Brr! It's getting
cold.

*THE SPOOK begins walking towards the house.*

TOM: Mr Gregory, what's that bell for?

THE SPOOK: Anyone who needs our help – anyone living
in fear of something they've seen in the dark
– will come to that bell. You'll hear it ring
many times, don't fret . . .

*Exit TOM and the Spook.*

# SCENE SIX

## THE SAME

*TOM is reading a note in the garden, puts down the paper and puts his head in his hands.*

*The daylight fades and the moon rises. An owl screeches and a breeze rustles the tree branches.*

*A figure in a long cloak enters, carrying a basket covered in cloth. It looks around, then rings the bell gently. A pause and it rings again.*

**ALICE** (*hisses*):   Tom. Tom!

*ALICE pulls down her hood and rings the bell again, more loudly.*

**TOM:**   Alice!

*TOM rushes over.*

**TOM:**   Shh! Keep it down will you? My master's sleeping.

**ALICE:**   Thought you'd forgotten.

**TOM:**   Course not.

*TOM is staring at ALICE's pointy shoes.*

**ALICE:**   I can see you're freaked out by my shoes –

first thing your master tells all his
apprentices. Silly old wives' tale, and he
should know better. Where I'm from, all the
girls wear them.

TOM (*gesturing to the basket*):
What's in there?

ALICE: They're for you, so that you can keep your
promise.

*TOM reaches out a hand to pull the cloth off the basket.*

ALICE: No, leave it be. Don't let the air get to them
or they'll spoil.

TOM: What are they?

ALICE: Just cakes.

TOM: But you wouldn't take one of mine. I thought
you wanted a favour.

ALICE: They're not for you.

*ALICE holds out the basket towards TOM.*

ALICE: These are for Old Mother Malkin.

*TOM takes a step back, away from the basket.*

TOM:    I don't think Mr Gregory would like it. He
        told me to keep away from that old witch.
        Took me down the garden and pointed her
        out to me especially.

ALICE:  He's a cruel man, Old Gregory. Poor Mother
        Malkin's been in that damp, dark hole for
        almost thirteen years, she has. Is it right to
        treat an old lady so badly?

TOM:    I don't know . . . She must have done
        something to deserve it.

ALICE:  Nothing but sweetness and light, she was,
        underneath it all. And whatever she done
        wrong, she's paid for it. Don't you think she
        deserves just a little treat . . . ?

*ALICE holds out the basket gently again and smiles at TOM.*
*TOM shakes his head and looks at the grave.*

ALICE:  Look, you won't get into trouble because Old
        Gregory need never know. It's only comfort
        you're bringing her. Her favourite cake made
        by her family. Ain't nothing wrong with that.
        Just something to keep up her strength
        against the cold. Gets right into her bones, it
        does. It's not right shoving an old lady in the
        ground and leaving her to rot. How would
        you feel if it was your grandmother?

TOM: I understand that, but . . . I can't . . . not without . . .

ALICE: Can't what? Oh, I see . . . you can't tell Gregory! I hear they've got some witch trouble in Pendle. He's gone, hasn't he? That's what's on that piece of paper, a farewell . . . ?

*TOM nods.*

ALICE: So he won't want you bothering him with little things like this. Don't you want him to think he can trust you?

TOM: I suppose so.

ALICE: If you don't do this, then there'll be many more of my clan after you. Trust me, just take the cakes. It's simple: just give her a cake each night. Three cakes for three nights. Best do it at midnight – it's then that she gets most peckish. Give her the first one tonight.

TOM (*sighing*): My dad always says you shouldn't make a promise you can't keep.

*TOM reaches out and takes the basket from ALICE.*

ALICE: You're a kind man, Tom Ward, not like your master. We could become good friends, you and me.

*ALICE exits, leaving TOM with the cakes.*

*The owl screeches*

TOM:            The full moon heavy on my head,
My soul is bursting, full of dread.
Here in my hands I hold the cakes,
Three night, three moons, is all it takes.

Would Alice fool me? She seems nice.
But these cakes smell like rats and mice,
And steam as though they're flaming hot.
You don't see cakes like this a lot.

The Spook warned me of pointy shoes,
But he does have old-fashioned views.
And if I give her a cake, just like Alice said,
My favour's done, and I can get back to bed.

Mother Malkin, can you hear me?

A spook's job is to keep the spirits down –
He's not the executioner of the town.
I only aim to do what I think's fair,
And Mam would want me to act like I care.

Mother Malkin?

*TOM holds out a cake over the pit.*

*The clock chimes midnight.*

Midnight strikes.
A promise, a word given.
I hope that if I'm wrong I'll be forgiven!

TOM *drops the cake into the pit.*

*Blackout.*

# SCENE SEVEN
## THE VILLAGE SQUARE

*A group of villagers and boys are gossiping. During
the following conversation others come and go, all
worried about what's happened.*

GROCER: Last night, I tell you. My wife heard
screaming from young Tommy's house, and
then this morning he was gone!

BAKER: Poor thing.

BUTCHER: Only seven years old. Didn't stand a chance
against a monster like that.

BOY 1: But what was it? Who saw it, Dad?

BUTCHER: Pipe down, boy! Or it'll be you she comes for
next.

SEAMSTRESS: Has anyone sent for the Spook?

TEACHER: Nobody's seen the Spook for days. Word is,
he's in Pendle, dealing with someone else's
witch.

BOY 2 (*whispering to Boy 1*):
Did you hear that?

GROCER: We need a search party. It don't take much

imagination to work out where Mother
Malkin's headed for.

**BOY 3** (*whispering*):
She's the worst! She'll chomp you down soon
as look at ya!

**SEAMSTRESS:** Surely it's not her! We haven't heard of her
since the last time the Spook trapped her. He
said she'd never trouble us again!

**BUTCHER:** Well, he was wrong, Maisie. Whatever the
Spook said, Mother Malkin has escaped. The
signs are unmistakable – a trail of slime and
the smell of rotting flesh from one side of the
village to the other.

**BOY 2** (*making the sign of the cross*):
Mother Malkin . . . no!

**BUTCHER:** Right! You lads, back to your houses, now!
There'll be no school today.

*The three boys exit hurriedly.*

**SEAMSTRESS:** May the Lord save that poor boy!

**GROCER:** Maisie, you go and comfort the boy's mother.
The rest of us will get together and come up
with a plan.

*There is shouting from offstage. The three boys re-enter, jostling TOM ahead of them.*

| | |
|---|---|
| **BOY 1:** | Look who we found, Dad! |
| **BOY 2:** | It'll be your fault then, Lefty. |
| **BOY 3:** | Murderer! |
| **BOY 2:** | I liked Tommy. Liked him more than you! |
| **BAKER:** | Boys, boys! What's going on here? Who is this poor lad? |
| **BOY 3:** | He's the Spook's apprentice! |
| **TEACHER:** | I remember him. Never could trust him . . . |
| **TOM:** | What's going on? What are you blaming me for? |
| **BOY 1:** | Little Tommy Brewer's been kidnapped. People say he's already been killed by her! |
| **BAKER:** | Now calm down, Arthur. Nobody knows that. |
| **TOM:** | Who's he been kidnapped by? |
| **BOY 2:** | By Mother Malkin! |

TOM: You're wrong. Mother Malkin's buried at the bottom of the Spook's garden.

SEAMSTRESS: That's what he told us, but her trail's been seen in the village.

BUTCHER: Some spook you'll be! Do you know anything about what you've let escape?

TOM (*despairing*):
She's evil. I've been told that much.

TEACHER: Evil doesn't even come close. She's called Mother Malkin because she likes children – but not to care for. She likes the *taste* of them. Uses their blood – innocent blood – for her magic. Mr Gregory found her squeezing the blood from a dead young 'un. He got her all right, but never Lizzie, her sidekick. And now both witches are free to murder again!

BOY 2: It's your fault! Spook should never have left you in charge of his business.

TOM: Don't worry, I'll get the boy back! I don't know what I'm going to do, but I'll sort it!

*All the villagers laugh.*

GROCER: Even if you could battle two witches, there's Tusk to face too. He's a product of the Fiend, they say. If I was you, I'd just hide. They'll come looking for you, I'm sure of it.

TOM: Where was Mother Malkin last seen? (*Impatient*) Where?

BAKER (*pointing*):
About half a mile outside the village, heading in that direction.

SEAMSTRESS: You be careful, Tom Ward!

TOM: Don't worry, I'll get the child back. And if you see Mr Gregory, tell him where I've gone!

*TOM exits, running.*

SEAMSTRESS: Good luck!

*Curtain.*

# ACT TWO

# SCENE ONE
## A PUBLIC HOUSE

*THE SPOOK is sitting by the fire with a glass of ale.*

*Enter a messenger, carrying a letter.*

MESSENGER: Are you John Gregory?

THE SPOOK: Aye, that's me. And who are you?

MESSENGER: I'm the poor man who's been roaming the County looking for you. Thought I'd drop dead before I delivered this letter! Asked at the coach 'ouses, asked at the inns, and always a step behind you. Beginning to think you were a ghost!

THE SPOOK: Stop complaining and tell me what you've come for! It's been a hard journey for me too, and I don't appreciate your bellowing.

MESSENGER: Got this message from a Tom Ward. Lad says you must read it, and I'm to wait for a response.

THE SPOOK: Spare my eyes and read it to me. For your rudeness you can earn your coin.

MESSENGER: Mind if I have a seat? My legs are weary.

THE SPOOK:      Do as you like – just read the letter!

*The messenger clears his throat.*

MESSENGER:      'Dear Master Celery' – sorry, 'Gregory'. Can't
                read his 'andwriting.

THE SPOOK:      Get on with it.

MESSENGER:      'Something terrible has happened. It's all got
                out of control and I don't know what to do.
                I've been fooled by one of the Deane clan
                and Mother Malkin has escaped—'

THE SPOOK:      What?! Carry on, lad. Tell me the rest,
                quickly.

MESSENGER:      'One of the boys from the village has been
                kidnapped and they're saying it's as food for
                her. Good news is, I got Mother Malkin in
                battle, down by the river.'

THE SPOOK:      Good lad!

MESSENGER:      'I took your cloak and the shortest staff I
                could find, and I tracked her by the trail of
                slime. By the time we were finished, I saw her
                float off dead in the water.'

THE SPOOK:      No! (*To the messenger*) Keep reading.

MESSENGER: 'I've tried to put everything right, but the villagers are baying for the Deane clan's blood. The boy hasn't been found yet, so I'm heading for Bony Lizzie's cottage now. I only hope I get there before the villagers burn it down. I need you back, Mr Gregory. Things are getting out of control. Every time I try to put it right, something else happens. Quick. Your faithful apprentice, Tom.'

THE SPOOK: Repeat one thing, lad. What did he say about Malkin?

MESSENGER: 'Floated off dead down a river', sir.

THE SPOOK: No, no, no!

MESSENGER: But he said *dead*.

THE SPOOK: Not a chance, lad! There are few ways to kill a witch, and drowning isn't one of them! He might have seen a corpse, but Malkin herself is not dead. That witch will find another host now.

MESSENGER: Host?

THE SPOOK: A new body, lad, flesh for Malkin to inhabit. That witch is alive!

MESSENGER: What message should I return with?

*THE SPOOK stands and flips the messenger a coin.*

**THE SPOOK:** None. I'll deliver it personally.

**MESSENGER:** Yes, sir.

**THE SPOOK:** Let's hope the horses are well rested – we've not a second to lose!

*Exit THE SPOOK and MESSENGER.*

# SCENE TWO
## BONY LIZZIE'S COTTAGE

*A sparsely furnished front room. On one side of the stage is the front door, on the other, the door to the kitchen and rest of the house. A fire burns at one end of the room, casting shadows onto the wall. BONY LIZZIE is sitting at a table, staring into a mirror, her face lit by candles. She breathes on the mirror and it seems to glow. Only MOTHER MALKIN's voice can be heard.*

**VOICE OF MOTHER MALKIN:**
　　　　Who calls me?

**BONY LIZZIE:**　Mother Malkin! Dear Mother Malkin, where are you? The clan have been waiting!

**VOICE OF MOTHER MALKIN:**
　　　　I am weak . . .

**BONY LIZZIE:**　Did you not receive the blood cakes? We have a child, ripe, and snatched from his mother, all ready for you.

**VOICE OF MOTHER MALKIN:**
　　　　No good, Lizzie! No good! The cakes were given, but the Spook tracked me down and I am without a body!

**BONY LIZZIE:**　But we got rid of Old Gregory. Our relatives distracted him with some nonsense about witch trouble in Pendle.

**VOICE OF MOTHER MALKIN:**
    Not him. The boy. His new apprentice.

**BONY LIZZIE:**   Tom Ward?

**VOICE OF MOTHER MALKIN:**
    Gave me the first two cakes, then got cold
    feet. But those were enough – I was strong
    enough to bend the bars of my pit and flee.
    But he followed. He *pursued* me.

**BONY LIZZIE:**   But some measly apprentice is no match for
    your—

**VOICE OF MOTHER MALKIN:**
    Shut it, Lizzie!

**BONY LIZZIE:**   Watch your tongue, Mother!

**VOICE OF MOTHER MALKIN:**
    If I only had a tongue! I have much to tell.
    But you must understand the need for
    revenge! Ward came at me very fast.

**BONY LIZZIE:**   They say he's brave.

**VOICE OF MOTHER MALKIN:**
    Brave, but he'll live to regret it! He gave me a
    blow with his staff, down by the riverbank.
    Knocked me clean into the stinking water.

**BONY LIZZIE:** The Mother Malkin I know wouldn't have given up!

**VOICE OF MOTHER MALKIN:**

I did not! He followed along as I floated – I could see his silhouette in the moonlight. I took him by surprise and sprang up, grabbing his ankle, my fingernails gouging into his flesh. So hard that his staff flew out of his hand. Agh! He should have been mine! He pulled me along the bank to where his wretched staff was, and then he gave me the fatal blow, crushing my skull to splinters.

**BONY LIZZIE:** Wretched boy! The Deane clan will make him pay. Will you find another host, Mother Malkin?

**VOICE OF MOTHER MALKIN:**

Of course I will. I don't know who yet, but be sure, I will find a body to possess. And when I do, it will be one perfectly placed for revenge!

*A huge roar shakes the walls of the room.*

**BONY LIZZIE:** I must go, Mother. Tusk must hunt.

**VOICE OF MOTHER MALKIN:**

Make Tusk strong, Lizzie, and be prepared for my return!

*There is a flash from the mirror, and MOTHER MALKIN is gone.*

**BONY LIZZIE:**   Alice! Where are you, useless toe-rag?

*ALICE emerges nervously through the door to the kitchen.*

**ALICE:**   Yes?

**BONY LIZZIE:**   Tusk must be fed. Look after the house while I'm gone, and don't let anyone in! Feed the child if you must.

**ALICE:**   Yes, Lizzie.

**BONY LIZZIE:**   Tusk! Walkies!

*Heavy footsteps shake the walls of the house. TUSK enters. He is enormous, bending low to enter the room. His mouth gapes, two large front teeth curving upwards over his top lip.*

**BONY LIZZIE:**   There's my big strong boy! It's time to go hunting. (*To Alice*) Remember what I said – if anything happens to Mother Malkin's dinner, it's you who'll take his place.

*LIZZIE crosses to the front door and opens it. TUSK barges past ALICE and follows her out, slamming the door behind him.*

*ALICE dashes to the window and watches them leave, then returns to the centre of the room.*

**ALICE:** Tommy? Tommy!

*ALICE goes off into the kitchen.*

**ALICE** (*off*): It's all right, they've gone. Are you hungry?

*TOMMY crawls out slowly from under the table. He is weak and scared.*

**ALICE** (*off*): It's just you and me now. Don't be frightened.

*ALICE re-enters from the kitchen, holding a plate of bread and butter.*

**ALICE:** There you are! Here, you must be famished.

*TOMMY grabs the plate from ALICE and starts to wolf down the food.*

**ALICE:** I'm sorry about the others.

**TOMMY:** You're not sorry. You tricked me into coming out into the garden at night. You're as bad as the rest of them!

**ALICE:** They made me do it! And if it wasn't you, it would be some other little boy!

*ALICE goes to TOMMY, but he scrambles away across the floor, his mouth full of bread.*

**TOMMY** (*starting to cry*):  I want my mummy . . .

*There is a banging on the front door. ALICE and TOMMY stop what they're doing and look at it. More banging.*

**TOM** (*off*):      Open up! I know you're in there! Alice? Alice!

*Banging continues.*

**TOMMY:**      Aren't you going to open it?

**ALICE:**      Go away – if you know what's good for you!

**TOMMY:**      Help! Help! I'm in here.

**TOM** (*off*):      Listen, you can open up now, or you can wait until the villagers get here and burn the whole place down.

**ALICE:**      Fine!

*ALICE undoes the latch and opens the front door. TOM barges past her into the room. He is wearing the Spook's cloak and carrying a staff.*

**TOM:**      Alice! How could you?

**ALICE:**      What do you want?

**TOM:**      You know what I want! I've come for the

child you and your family of witches have
stolen! I was so stupid to trust you!

ALICE:          Don't be a fool, Tom. Go away before it's too
                late. They could be back at any minute, and
                once Tusk gets your scent, you've had it.

TOM:            I don't care. I've killed Mother Malkin, I can
                kill Bony Lizzie too!

*TOM goes to TOMMY and comforts him.*

TOM:            You must be Tommy. Don't worry, there's no
                need to be afraid. I'm going to take you home
                to your mam.

*TOM scoops TOMMY into his arms.*

TOMMY:          I'm frightened.

TOM:            You're safe now. We've got the same name. My
                name is Tommy too. Now let's get you home.

*TOM tries to walk past ALICE with the child, but Alice holds her
ground. They are face to face.*

ALICE:          You're a fool, Tom. Give him back before it's
                too late.

TOM:            I'd rather be a fool than do the dirty work of
                witches.

TOM *barges past ALICE and out of the door.*

**ALICE** (*shouting after him*):

> They'll come after you! You'll never get away!

ALICE *lets out a shriek of anger.*

# SCENE THREE

## THE WARD FAMILY HOME

*DAD and JACK are looking out towards the horizon.
Smoke in the distance.*

DAD:      Must be coming from the village.

JACK:      If one house went up in flames down there, the lot would be gone. There's not enough smoke for that.

DAD:      Maybe it's one of those houses out on its own, then.

JACK:      Poor devils, whoever they are. I can smell the burning timber from 'ere.

*Enter MAM.*

MAM:      Aren't you two coming in for dinner?

JACK:      Stop nagging, Mam! We'll come when we're ready.

DAD:      Don't speak to your mother like that! Honest, Jack, your temper these days ... (*To Mam*) Smoke on the horizon, love.

MAM:      Well I'll be ...

*ELLIE enters, cradling a newborn baby.*

JACK: Don't bring Mary out here! She'll get her lungs all full of smoke.

MAM: Don't be silly, Jack! That fire's miles away. And it's better for her to be out here than inside with the cooking smoke.

DAD: Look at our son, all protective of his young 'un!

*MAM goes to ELLIE and takes the baby from her.*

MAM: Would you look at the nose on her! She's a Ward if ever I saw one!

JACK: Mary's the most beautiful baby in the whole County. Not surprising with a mother like Ellie.

ELLIE (*shyly*): Stop it, Jack ...

MAM: Reminds me of our Tom when he was a baby. But he had such a serious face.

DAD: And now he's off fighting who knows what evil—, and who's to say when he'll be back? You look away for a moment and they've all grown up.

MAM:        Come on now. Think of the good he's doing.

JACK:        I'm sure Tom will come home as soon as he can, Dad.

ELLIE:        Oh!

JACK:        Ellie!

*ELLIE has half fainted. She is crouched, trying to get her vision back.*

DAD:        What's the matter?

*The whole family have gathered around ELLIE, fussing over her.*

ELLIE:        It's nothing, really. I just felt strange for a moment.

MAM:        Just as well I was holding the baby!

JACK:        Let's go inside and eat. It's our fault for keeping dinner waiting.

ELLIE:        I just feel so dizzy these last few days.

MAM:        Come on, all of you. Wash those hands and we'll sit down together.

*The others go into the house. MAM is left holding the baby, looking towards the plume of smoke.*

MAM:            Oh, Mary. Why do I get the feeling Tom's got
                something to do with this?

JACK (*off*):    Mam, the meat's burning!

MAM:            I'm coming!

*MAM goes into the house.*

# SCENE FOUR
## OUTSIDE THE SPOOK'S GARDEN

*ALICE is standing in the shade, ringing the Spook's bell.*
*TOM hurries out of the house to meet her.*

**TOM** (*angry*):    What are *you* doing here?

**ALICE:**    I've come to say goodbye. And to warn you never to go walking near Pendle. That's where we're going. Lizzie has family living there.

**TOM** (*softening*):    I'm glad you escaped. I saw the smoke when they burned down your house.

**ALICE:**    Lizzie knew they were coming, so we got away with plenty of time to spare. She knows what you did to Mother Malkin. Didn't sniff you out at all, and that worries her. She said your shadow had a funny smell.

*TOM laughs.*

**ALICE:**    Ain't funny. Ain't nothing to laugh at. She only smelled your shadow where it had fallen on the wall. It showed the truth of you.

*ALICE takes a step towards TOM, into the sunlight.*

**ALICE** (*wrinkling her nose*):
    She's right. You do smell funny.

TOM: Look, don't go to Pendle. You're better off without them. Those witches are just bad company.

*ALICE steps back, looking afraid.*

ALICE: Bad company don't matter to me. Won't change me, will it? I'm bad already. Bad inside. You wouldn't believe the things I've done.

TOM: What are you talking about?

ALICE: I'm sorry, I've been bad again. I'm just not strong enough to say no.

*Suddenly TUSK appears behind TOM and throws a sack over him. TOM struggles, but TUSK picks him up and throws him over his shoulder.*

ALICE: Tusk! No, that wasn't what we agreed!

TUSK (*grunts*): Agree? No agree. Lizzie's orders. My job!

ALICE: It was just supposed to be a warning for him to stay away. That's what we said!

TUSK (*grabbing her arm*):
Careful, girl. Don't give me orders. I work for clan.

*TUSK throws ALICE to the floor.*

**TUSK:** Not for you!

**ALICE** (*sobbing*): Please! It's going too far, too far!

**TUSK:** Clan be . . . ashamed of you.

*TUSK exits, leaving ALICE crying. After a moment she wipes her eyes and shouts after him.*

**ALICE:** Be careful with him!

*ALICE exits.*

# SCENE FIVE
## THE VILLAGE SQUARE

*Dusk. The MIDWIFE and BAKER stand talking with
TOMMY between them. THE SPOOK enters hurriedly,
messenger following him reluctantly.*

**THE SPOOK** (*hurriedly*):

I'm looking for my apprentice. Have you seen
him?

**MIDWIFE:**    Are you talking about young Tom?

**THE SPOOK:**    That's right, Tom Ward.

**MIDWIFE:**    Oh, the hero of the village!

**BAKER:**    A fine young lad, Mr Gregory. Really, you
must be very proud of him.

**THE SPOOK:**    That's all well and good, but have you seen
him?

**MIDWIFE:**    Snatched my Tommy from the jaws of a
witch.

**BAKER:**    Broke down her door and snatched him from
her plate – that's what I heard.

**TOMMY:**    I like Tom – he carried me all the way home.

| | |
|---|---|
| **THE SPOOK:** | And for that he shall be duly rewarded. But will one of you please tell me where he is! |
| **MIDWIFE:** | Poor boy must be exhausted after what he's been through, looking after things while you were off doing goodness knows what. |
| **THE SPOOK:** | Listen, the lad is in great danger and needs my help. If you don't help me find him, he won't be a hero any more. He'll be dead – crushed between the jaws of the most evil witch the County has ever seen! What's more, you'll be next! |

*Pause – the villagers shocked.*

(*To the messenger*) Boy, ride on ahead to my cottage and ring the bell. I'll follow you on foot.

*The messenger sighs and exits.*

(*To others*): Tell the rest of the village there's a witch on the loose. And whatever you do, don't let your children go outside!

*THE SPOOK exits. MIDWIFE, BAKER and TOMMY run off in the opposite direction.*

# SCENE SIX
## A BLEAK HILLSIDE

*TOM is tied to a tree, guarded by BONY LIZZIE and TUSK.*
*ALICE skulks nearby, looking terrified.*

**BONY LIZZIE** (*to Tusk*):

There, we've got him safe enough. (*To Tom*)
Well, boy. How does it feel to know that
you'll never see the light of day again?

*LIZZIE is inches from TOM's face. He winces at the smell.*

**BONY LIZZIE:** You won't cross any more witches.

**TOM:** I've been in worse situations! I've survived
a ghast trying to bury me and I'll survive
you!

**BONY LIZZIE:** You're wasting your useless breath!

**ALICE** (*hisses*): Please, Tom, you need to be quiet!

**BONY LIZZIE:** Why do you talk to him like that? Quiet
yourself and your snivelling concern! (*To
Tom*) Anything I can get for you, Ward?
What about a nice warm drink?

*TUSK holds TOM while LIZZIE pours some liquid down his*
*throat. TOM squirms desperately and spits it out.*

**BONY LIZZIE:** Spit at me again, boy, and I'll make your agony slower!

*LIZZIE pinches his nose and pours again.*

**TOM:** Argh! Make them stop, Alice! Please!

**BONY LIZZIE:** There now, that'll keep your eyes wide open. Wouldn't want you dozing off, would we? Wouldn't want you to miss a thing. Tusk! Time for a quick hunt. You'll need all your strength tonight.

**TUSK:** Enjoy your last night on this earth, boy.

*LIZZIE leaves, taking TUSK with her. ALICE goes to kneel by TOM.*

**ALICE:** I never meant for this to happen, Tom. If only you hadn't meddled, it would have been all right.

**TOM:** Been all right? If you'd had your way, another child would be dead by now. And the Spook too. Those cakes had the blood of a baby inside. Do you call that being all right? You come from a family of murderers – you're a murderer yourself!

**ALICE:** Ain't true. It ain't true, that! I didn't know about no baby until they'd got him. All I did was give you the cakes.

TOM:          You knew what they were going to do
              afterwards. And you would've let it happen.

ALICE:        I ain't that strong, Tom. How could I stop it?
              How could I stop Lizzie?

TOM:          We all have to choose whether to do good or
              bad in life. I've made my choice. But what
              will you do? Be strong now, Alice!

ALICE:        Ain't choosing neither. I don't want to be like
              them. I'll run away. As soon as I get the
              chance, I'll be off.

TOM:          Then help me now! Help me to get out of
              this, and we could run away together.

ALICE:        No – it's too dangerous now. But when they
              ain't expecting it, maybe weeks from now,
              then I'll be gone.

TOM:          You mean, after I'm dead? When you've got
              more blood on your hands?

*ALICE looks away and begins to cry softly. Suddenly she gets up
and listens carefully.*

ALICE:        Oh, Tom, I'm sorry! I can hear Lizzie
              sharpening her knives!

TOM:          If you're really sorry, you'll help me!

**ALICE** (*crying*):  Ain't nothing I can do. Lizzie could turn on me. She don't trust me anyway. Thinks I'm soft.

**TOM:**  Then go and find help. Find Mr Gregory and bring him here!

**ALICE:**  Too late for that, ain't it? Lizzie's a bone witch. Bones taken in daylight are no use to her. No use at all. She wants your bones, and the best time to take them is just before the sun comes up. They'll be coming for you in a few minutes. That's all the time you've got.

**TOM:**  Then get me a knife.

**ALICE:**  We can't fight 'em, Tom! Tusk's too strong.

**TOM:**  No, I want it to cut the rope. I think if I had a chance I could at least outrun them.

*ALICE looks at TOM for a moment, then glances offstage.*

**TOM:**  Please, Alice. I won't let them hurt you.

*ALICE runs off quickly to a pile of LIZZIE's belongings. TOM starts struggling against the ropes.*

*ALICE rushes back holding a knife, which she tries to put in TOM's hands.*

**ALICE:**        You've only got moments. Hurry!

**TOM:**        You'll have to do it for me. Come on – please, Alice.

*ALICE starts trying to cut TOM's hands free.*

**BONY LIZZIE** (*offstage*):
        My knives will treat his body like butter, Tusk!

**TOM:**        Quickly, Alice!

**TUSK** (*offstage*):  Cry like an infant, he will!

**ALICE** (*struggling*):
        I'm trying!

**BONY LIZZIE** (*nearer*):
        The Deane clan's moment has finally come!

**TOM:**        Alice!

*BONY LIZZIE and TUSK enter.*

**BONY LIZZIE** (*seeing Alice*):
        You wretched girl! What do you think you're doing?

**TUSK:**        Traitor!

**BONY LIZZIE:** I've had enough of this. If you're so fond of that meddling boy, you can share his fate! Tusk, grab her!

**ALICE:** No!

*TUSK moves towards ALICE as she scrambles backwards on all fours.*

*THE SPOOK enters. ALICE backs straight into his legs.*

**THE SPOOK:** Hello, Lizzie.

*TUSK stops and turns to LIZZIE for instructions.*

**BONY LIZZIE:** No!

**THE SPOOK:** That Pendle story was a good distraction, but you should have chosen somewhere further away.

**BONY LIZZIE:** You're too late, Gregory. Mother Malkin's on the loose and once she has a body, no child in the County will be safe.

**THE SPOOK:** Maybe, but this is one boy who won't be her victim.

**TUSK:** Why you so sure, old man?

**THE SPOOK:** It's time for the chain, Lizzie.

**BONY LIZZIE:**   No! Get him, Tusk!

**TUSK:**        Tusk hungry!

*TUSK begins to launch himself towards THE SPOOK. ALICE presses her face against the tree and TOM strains against the ropes. THE SPOOK pulls his hand from his pocket in a tight fist. He throws a handful of dust into the centre of the stage.*

*There is a loud bang, a puff of smoke and blackout.*

# SCENE SEVEN
## THE SAME

*As the lights fade up, THE SPOOK is standing on guard, his staff held across his chest. TOM and ALICE stand cautiously behind him. On the floor in front of him are TUSK, unconscious, and LIZZIE, bound by a silver chain.*

**THE SPOOK** (*poking Tusk with his staff*):
Aye, that's done for him.

*LIZZIE is struggling against the chain, but it's tight around her mouth.*

**TOM:** How did you find us?

**THE SPOOK:** There are signs, lad. Trails that can be followed, if you know how. And when the boggart let me know it'd seen you go out to the bell, I knew where to look first. All skills you'll learn in good time.

*THE SPOOK turns to ALICE and stares at her intently.*

**THE SPOOK:** That's two of them dealt with, but what are we going to do about you?

**TOM:** She tried to help me escape.

**THE SPOOK:** Is that so? But what else did she do? Open your mouth, girl. I want to see your teeth.

*ALICE obeys and approaches THE SPOOK with her mouth
open. He grabs her jaw and sniffs loudly.*

**THE SPOOK** (*releasing Alice*):

Her breath is sweet enough. You've smelled
the other one's breath?

*TOM nods.*

**THE SPOOK:** It's caused by her diet, and it tells you right
away what she's been up to. Those who
practise bone or blood magic get a taste for
raw meat. But the girl seems all right.

*THE SPOOK moves closer to ALICE again.*

**THE SPOOK:** Look into my eyes, girl! Hold my gaze as long
as you can.

*ALICE looks into THE SPOOK's eyes for a few seconds, then
turns away, sobbing.*

**THE SPOOK** (*shaking his head*):

I don't know what's for the best. It's not just
her. We've others to think about. Innocents
who might suffer in the future. She's seen too
much and she knows too much for her own
good. I don't know if it's safe to let her go. If
she goes east to join the brood at Pendle,
she'll be lost for ever, only adding to the dark.

TOM:     Haven't you anywhere else you could go,
        Alice? No other relations?

ALICE:     There's a village near the coast. It's called
        Staumin. I've another aunt who lives there.
        Perhaps she'd take me in.

THE SPOOK:   Is she like the others?

ALICE:     She'd never hurt anyone. Please, Mr Gregory.

THE SPOOK (*softening*):
        Very well. I'm going to give you one chance,
        girl. It's up to you whether you use it wisely.
        If you don't, then one day we'll meet again
        and I shan't be so charitable. (*Turning to
        Tom*) But first, I want you to take the girl
        back to your family's farm, lad. Let your
        mother talk to her. I've a feeling she might
        just be able to help. What do you reckon?

TOM (*looks at ALICE, then nods at THE SPOOK*):
        I'll do that. Thank you, sir.

THE SPOOK (*looking over at LIZZIE*):
        Now then, I've got a pit to dig.

# SCENE EIGHT
## OUTSIDE THE WARD FAMILY FARM

*SNOUT is sharpening a long blade on a leather strop.*
*TOM and ALICE enter.*

TOM (*to Alice*): Better wait here. I'll go in and explain. Dad'll be out in the fields, but Mam will be in the kitchen.

SNOUT: Well, if it isn't the long-lost son!

TOM: Hello, Snout.

SNOUT: What brings you back to this humble abode, Master Tom?

*TOM walks straight past SNOUT towards the door of the house.*

TOM: Nothing. Just family business.

SNOUT: Stop!

*TOM stops and turns back, shocked.*

SNOUT: I mean, spare a moment for a friend of the family, Tom. Far be it from me, a lowly slaughterman, to pry. It's just been so long.

TOM: I'm sorry, Snout, I didn't mean to be rude. How are you?

SNOUT:       Might just keep this message I've been
             carrying to myself.

TOM:         I need to speak to Mam, that's all. I'm sorry.

SNOUT:       Apology accepted. Might surprise you to
             know I were expecting you to turn up.
             Happened to pass your master on the road
             this morning. He said you're to hold tight
             and wait here till he comes and gets you.
             Whatever happens, stay here and don't go on
             as planned. Just stay here with company.

TOM:         That's strange. I wonder what made him
             change his mind . . .

*Pause. ALICE is skulking, observing SNOUT suspiciously.*

SNOUT:       Sure it's nothing to worry about. Anyway,
             why're you stood here chatting away to me?
             Didn't you hear there's a new Ward in the
             world for you to meet?

TOM:         Of course – Ellie! The baby's come!

*SNOUT laughs to himself.*

ALICE:       What's so funny?

SNOUT:       I'm not in the way of talking about *new* life
             normally. I'm here to take it away!

*SNOUT is laughing so hard his hand slips past the strop and he drops his heavy knife on the ground.*

SNOUT:        Oops, silly me. Now, where are those pigs?

*TOM and ALICE watch SNOUT leave. MAM comes out of the house.*

MAM:        Well I never! What are you doing here?

*TOM rushes to MAM and hugs her. ALICE looks down, embarrassed.*

MAM:        We weren't expecting you home till autumn!

*MAM sees ALICE.*

MAM:        Oh. Tom, when you bring a guest with you, it's good manners to introduce them. I thought I'd taught you better than that.

TOM:        Mam, this is Alice. Mr Gregory told me to bring her here so you could talk to her. Alice has been . . . keeping bad company. I thought it best to tell you what's happened first, just in case . . . well, in case you thought it was better she didn't—

*JACK and ELLIE enter, ELLIE carrying BABY MARY.*

**ELLIE:**     Tom! I've got someone who wants to meet you.

*TOM goes over to see the baby.*

**TOM:**     I can't believe it. It's so small!

**JACK:**     It's a 'she'. And she's called Mary.

**ELLIE:**     You should have seen her when she was first born – Jack could hold her in the palm of his hand! It's good to see you, Tom.

**MAM:**     Alice, why don't you come inside with me. Leave Tom to get better acquainted with his new niece, eh. Go on.

*MAM gestures to ALICE, who goes into the house.*

**MAM:**     Tom, word got back to us about what happened.

**TOM** (*looking down*):
          Oh.

**MAM:**     You've done well, son. You're young and new to the job, so mistakes can be forgiven. We're just happy to see you safe, that's all.

*MAM exits.*

ELLIE: Oh dear, Tom, I must look a mess. I've been up all night. I've just managed an hour's sleep. You've got to take it when you can with a hungry baby like this. She cries a lot – especially at night.

TOM: How old is she?

ELLIE: She'll be just six days old tonight. She was born not long after midnight last Saturday. I expect you were tucked up in bed, oblivious!

TOM: No, that was the night I . . . It doesn't matter.

*From the kitchen comes the sound of ALICE and MAM laughing.*

ELLIE: Who is that with your mam?

TOM: It's Alice – my friend . . . I'll explain later. Baby Mary is lovely. I'm so pleased for you.

ELLIE: Oh dear. Jack? I've suddenly come over a bit faint again.

JACK (*going to her*):
Go inside and sit down. It's Tom's fault – getting everyone excited, turning up unannounced.

ELLIE: Thanks, love. See you later, Tom.

*JACK helps ELLIE back into the house, then turns to face TOM.*

**TOM:**  It's good to see you too, Jack.

**JACK:**  Who's the girl?

**TOM:**  She's just someone who needs help. The Spook told me to bring her here so that Mam could talk to her.

**JACK:**  What do you mean, she needs help?

**TOM:**  She's been keeping bad company, that's all.

**JACK** (*stepping closer*):
  What sort of bad company?

**TOM:**  Her aunt is a witch, but don't worry – the Spook has sorted it out and we'll only be staying a few days. Then he'll come and collect us.

**JACK:**  Don't you have the sense you were born with? Didn't you think? Didn't you think about the baby? There's an innocent child living in this house and you're bringing in someone from a family like that! It's beyond belief!

**TOM:**  Mam's fine with it, why can't you be?

JACK:     Mam's too kind-hearted for her own good. That Spook has changed you and your priorities with a load of stupid ideas! When Dad gets back from market, you see how tired he looks – this is the last thing he needs. He's finding the job harder and harder . . . You'll have to earn your keep while you're here.

TOM:     Of course I'll help, and so will Alice!

JACK:     Good. And if she so much as looks at our baby funny, I'm holding you responsible!

*JACK exits, leaving TOM alone.*

# SCENE NINE
## ALICE'S BEDROOM

*ALICE (off): Goodnight! Thank you for dinner.*
*It was nice to meet you all!*

*ALICE enters looking happy. She bustles around the room,*
*unpacking her clothes. There is the screech of an owl from outside*
*her window. Suddenly ALICE stops and looks towards the*
*window, breathing in slowly through her nose. She crosses to the*
*door and listens intently. We can hear the murmur of voices from*
*downstairs. ALICE looks at the mirror on her dressing table.*

**ALICE** (*to herself*): Where are you, Mother Malkin?

*ALICE sits down at the dressing table and lights a candle. She*
*breathes on the mirror and draws a strange pattern in the*
*condensation. The glass begins to glow green.*

**ALICE:**     Whether in sickness,
               whether in health,
               in this mirror show yourself.

**VOICE OF MOTHER MALKIN** (*weakly*):
               Who calls?

*ALICE shuts her eyes.*

**VOICE OF MOTHER MALKIN:**
               *Who calls? Lizzie, is that you?* It took time to
               choose a host, but I have found one. I am
               close by the Ward boy's house.

91

*ALICE gasps, then claps her hand over her mouth.*

**VOICE OF MOTHER MALKIN** (*angrily*):
Who's there? Speak! Who dares summon
Mother Malkin?

**ALICE** (*unable to help herself*):
You'll never take their baby!

**VOICE OF MOTHER MALKIN:**
*Wretched* girl. Treacherous weakling!

*ALICE moves to snuff out the candle, but her hand is stopped. She struggles to move.*

**ALICE:**   Let me go!

**VOICE OF MOTHER MALKIN:**
Consider this a warning, child. Do not try to
stop me.

**ALICE** (*struggling to breathe*):
Help . . .

**VOICE OF MOTHER MALKIN:**
My power over this body grows hourly. When
I have fully possessed it, revenge will be
mine!

**ALICE:**   I won't let you—

**VOICE OF MOTHER MALKIN:**
Stand in my way and suffer for it!

*There is a knock on the bedroom door and TOM enters immediately.*

**TOM:** I just wanted to say goodnight, Alice. We've got a busy day t—

*TOM sees ALICE and the glowing mirror.*

**VOICE OF MOTHER MALKIN:**
The time is approaching.

*TOM grabs a candlestick, and with a roar slams it into the mirror, smashing it. ALICE falls to the floor.*

**TOM:** Alice! Alice, how could you?

**ALICE:** No, Tom, I only wanted to see—

*JACK comes running in, disturbed by the noise.*

**JACK:** What's going on here? Tom! Do you know how old that mirror was?

**TOM:** I'm sorry, Jack. I had to do it.

**JACK:** What do you think Dad will say now? How will he feel when he gets back and sees this?

TOM:   You don't understand.

JACK:   How dare you . . .

*ELLIE enters just as JACK moves to strike TOM. She is carrying*
*BABY MARY.*

ELLIE:   No, Jack, don't! What good will that do?

JACK:   What has got into you? First you take Dad's
      tinderbox, his prized possession, and now
      you smash his family heirloom. What are you
      doing in here anyway?

TOM:   We need to speak to Mam, Jack. Where is she?

JACK:   She's been called out to help with a difficult
      birth in the village. And you can think
      yourself lucky she has! Might not be back
      until morning.

*ELLIE is leaning against the wall.*

ELLIE:   Jack, I need you to take the baby.

JACK:   Of course, love. (*He does so*) Tom, stay in
      your own room from now on. I've a good
      mind to send the pair of you packing this
      second. (*To Ellie*) I'll put her back to bed.

*JACK exits.*

TOM: How could you, Alice? I trusted you . . .

ELLIE: What's all this about, Tom? If there's some danger here, you need to tell us now.

ALICE: Tom, listen to me. I only used the mirror because—

TOM (*harshly*): Save it! I should never have trusted you.

*ALICE sits with her head in her hands.*

ELLIE: What's the problem, Tom? You can tell me. I know you're a sensible lad, and you must have had a reason for what you did.

TOM: There is something, Ellie. But I don't know how to start.

ELLIE: Start at the beginning.

TOM: I broke the mirror because I think some evil has followed me here. A witch. Alice was talking to her and—

ELLIE (*suddenly furious*):
Tell Jack that, and you would certainly feel his fist! You mean you've brought something back here, when I've got a new baby to care for? How could you? How could you do that?

TOM:      You need to leave the house and take the baby to safety. Go now, before it's too late!

ELLIE:      You expect us to take a child out at this time of night?

TOM:      I think you have to.

ELLIE:      Jack wouldn't leave. He wouldn't be driven out of his own house in the middle of the night. Not by anything. I'm going to stay here too, and I'm going to say my prayers. The Lord will protect us. Anyway, you could be wrong, Tom. You're still inexperienced – just an apprentice.

TOM:      I hope so.

ELLIE:      Your mam will be back in the morning. In the meantime, keep out of here, Tom. (*Looking at Alice*) There's something not right about her.

*ELLIE exits.*

ALICE:      You have to listen to me.

*TOM turns to ALICE.*

TOM:      I don't want to talk to you, Alice. You've had your chance. I just want you to leave!

ALICE: You'd better talk to me if you know what's good for you. Soon it'll be too late. Mother Malkin's already here.

TOM: I know that – I saw you talking to her!

ALICE: Not just in the mirror, though. It ain't just that. She's *here*, Tom, she's somewhere close by. Maybe even inside the house. And she's getting stronger.

TOM: You brought her here. You told her where I was.

ALICE: Ain't true! I sensed her and sniffed her out, then I used the mirror to see where she was. Didn't realize she was so close, did I? Lucky you came in when you did. She was too strong for me – I couldn't break away from her. Lucky for me you smashed that mirror.

TOM: We'll wait here for Mr Gregory to arrive. He'll know what to do.

ALICE: Ain't time for that. There's Jack and Ellie's baby to think about. Mother Malkin wants to hurt you, yes, but she'll be hungry for young blood – it's what she likes best. That's what makes her strongest.

| TOM: | Baby Mary! What can I do? What chance have I got against Mother Malkin? Ellie's right: I'm only an apprentice. |
|---|---|
| ALICE: | Don't sleep tonight. Watch and listen carefully for anything unusual. I'll do the same. |
| TOM: | How will we find her? |
| ALICE: | I don't know, Tom, but we'd better think of something. Because if she finds us first, there'll be more things than mirrors broken. |

# SCENE TEN
## OUTSIDE THE WARD FAMILY FARM

*ALICE is waiting anxiously outside the house.*

ALICE:        Come on, Mrs Ward . . . We need your help.

*TOM enters, carrying his bag of belongings.*

ALICE:        Tom! Where are you going?

TOM:        I'm going back to Chipenden to find Mr
Gregory. We need help urgently, so I'd better
go and fetch him myself.

ALICE:        But what about Baby Mary? Tom, you can't
just leave us all here. You're the Spook's
apprentice!

TOM:        You said Mother Malkin was getting stronger.
Maybe I've time to find the Spook and come
back before she's ready to make her move.

ALICE:        You can't risk it.

TOM:        Anyway, it's me she wants revenge on. If she
knows I've left, maybe she'll follow. Hanging
around here is only asking for trouble. I'm
putting you all in danger.

ALICE:        No, she'll wait for you. After thirteen years in a grave, she's learned patience if not forgiveness. You'll come back to find Baby Mary gone and Mother Malkin stronger than ever.

*TOM throws down his bag and sits on the tree stump, head in hands.*

TOM:              Then what can I do? It's hopeless. If I stay here, I won't be able to fight Mother Malkin, and if I leave, I give her exactly what she needs.

ALICE:            You're sure you can't think of anything else?

*TOM shakes his head.*

ALICE:            Surely Old Gregory taught you something that could be useful? If you didn't write it down in that notebook of yours, then maybe it's inside your head? Search!

TOM:              He's not said that much yet about witches; we've mostly been studying boggarts and ghasts.

ALICE:            Well, I'm sure he didn't say anything about running off. *Think*, Tom.

*Pause. TOM racks his brains.*

TOM:        Wait, he did say something about possession. He said . . .

ALICE:      Come on, Tom!

TOM:        He said there's two signs. First is . . . dizziness.

ALICE:      Well done!

TOM:        But wait – Ellie keeps feeling faint . . . Surely she can't be—

ALICE:      You can't be sure, Tom. She's just had a baby, and that's bound to make her feel weak. What's the second?

TOM:        My master said that a witch is desperate to hang onto her new body, and that puts her in a terrible temper. Well, that sounds like our Jack, doesn't it?

ALICE:      You know him better than I do.

TOM:        He's been worse since I came home. But I suppose he always did have his moods. Oh, Alice, it's so hard to know!

ALICE:      Keep thinking, Tom. I'd better get back inside. I promised your mam before she left last night that I'd help prepare the chicken for lunch. And I think we should make things seem as normal as possible, don't you? Your dad's still sleeping off yesterday's work, and I don't think we should wake him until we have to. Do you know where your mam keeps the salt and pepper?

TOM: That's it!

ALICE: What?

TOM: I knew there was something else! Salt and iron! Mr Gregory told me that all spooks use salt and iron to bind witches. It's what he used on Lizzie. Dad's bound to have some iron filings in the workshop, and there's plenty of salt in the kitchen. If Mother Malkin does surprise us, we'll have a weapon.

ALICE: Go and fill your pockets, Tom! I'll wait here in case your mam comes home. Hurry!

*TOM runs into the house. ALICE paces, looking out for MAM.*

ALICE: I'll not be your messenger any more, Pendle witches. I don't want to be bad. I like it here with these people, and if you want me back that much, you'll have to drag me home. No more magic. No more children. I don't want anyone to get hurt. (*Repeating under her breath*) No more magic, no more children. No more magic, no more—

*A cry of pain comes from round the corner of the house. ALICE looks in that direction.*

ALICE:          No, we're too late!

*JACK runs on, covered in blood, clutching his stomach.*

JACK:           Where's Tom?

ALICE:          He went to the workshop. What happened?

*JACK exits into the house.*

ALICE:          It's all my fault, it's all my fault. She wouldn't
                be here if I hadn't given him the blood cakes.
                Why do I always have to do what they tell
                me?

*ELLIE enters slowly from round the side of the house, her hands clutched to her mouth, her back to ALICE.*

ALICE:          Ellie? What's the matter? Ellie, what's wrong?

*ELLIE continues to walk backwards, trembling.*

ALICE:          It's like someone's controlling you.

*ELLIE stumbles and falls to the ground.*

ALICE:          It *is* you! Mother Malkin's taken over your
                body.

*ALICE goes over to ELLIE and takes her fiercely by the shoulders. TOM and JACK re-enter.*

**TOM:**        Alice!

**JACK:**        What's happened to Ellie?

**ALICE:**        It's her, Tom! Mother Malkin's possessed her! (*To Ellie*) Can you hear me, you vile creature?

**JACK:**        No!

**ALICE:**        Quick, Tom, use the salt and iron!

**TOM:**        You're wrong. It's not Ellie . . . No, it doesn't feel right.

**ALICE:**        Who then, Tom? Quick!

**TOM:**        Of course! Remember Snout's words – 'I'm not in the way of talking about *new* life normally. I'm here to take it away!' He said the words, but it was Malkin who told us herself – it's Snout she's possessed! I can hear him coming. I'll talk to him, you keep on his blindside!

*ALICE nods.*

*ELLIE screams. SNOUT comes round the corner of the house,*

*carrying his long curved knife and baby MARY. He is smiling*
*menacingly. SNOUT speaks in mother malkin's voice.*

SNOUT:          Come here, boy! Come to me. (*Laughing*)
                Think you're trained to fight the dark? Ha!
                Rubbish. Life for a life. Now come closer,
                Tom Ward. I want *your* blood. You can save
                this little one.

*TOM starts to walk towards SNOUT. We see him trying to stop,*
*to stay where he is, but MOTHER MALKIN is controlling him.*
*SNOUT is holding the knife out, ready to strike.*

ALICE:          Tom, it's a spell. She's compelled you! Fight
                it! Stop, please! (*Getting louder*) Tom? Tom!
                Tom!

*ALICE leaps at SNOUT, kicking him and snatching the baby as*
*he falls back. SNOUT is doubled over, gasping in pain.*

TOM (*coming out of his trance*):
                Alice! Are you OK? How's the baby?

ALICE:          Fine, Tom. She's fine.

*ALICE takes the baby over to ELLIE and JACK.*

TOM (*to Snout*): I *am* trained to fight the dark. You were
                wrong to underestimate me!

SNOUT:          Worthless little apprentice!

*TOM digs into his pockets and pulls out a handful of iron filings in one hand and salt in the other.*

**TOM:** Goodbye, Malkin.

*TOM throws the handfuls together at SNOUT's face.*

*SNOUT collapses on the floor with a yelp. There is a puff of smoke and a flash, and MOTHER MALKIN appears on stage next to SNOUT's body. MOTHER MALKIN is wriggling in pain from the iron and salt. ALICE picks up a short branch from the ground and crosses to TOM.*

**ALICE:** Tom, you'll need this. Pass me your tinderbox.

**MOTHER MALKIN** (*gasping*):
Traitor to your family, Alice Deane! It is you who will burn in hell for this!

*TOM pulls the tinderbox from his pocket, but hesitates.*

**TOM:** Alice, I can't burn her. She's harmless now. Look at her, she's beaten!

**MOTHER MALKIN:**
Gregory bound me, never killed me, boy. Have mercy!

**ALICE** (*to Tom*): Get harder or you won't survive! Just doing what Old Gregory says won't be enough. You'll die – just like the other apprentices before you! You have to burn a witch, to make sure she don't come back. Putting her in the ground ain't no good. It just delays things. Old Gregory knows that, but he's too soft to use burning.

ELLIE:        Tom!

*MOTHER MALKIN has taken advantage of TOM and ALICE's distraction and is scurrying away, offstage.*

ALICE:        Now it's too late.

TOM:          No, she's weak.

*TOM takes the branch from ALICE and runs after MOTHER MALKIN. There is a crash as farm tools are kicked, the squelching of mud, then MOTHER MALKIN screams again and we hear the squeals of pigs. Then final silence.*

*TOM re-enters. Everyone looks at him.*

TOM:          I don't think she'll be back.

ALICE:        Did you . . . ?

TOM:          Her pointed feet got stuck in the mud. I didn't have to do anything.

SNOUT (*still on the floor, but conscious again*):
              It sounds like the pigs have had the lot of her.

107

*ELLIE is sobbing, holding baby MARY.*

JACK:    Ellie, it's over now. Don't worry, love.

ELLIE:    Horrible. It was horrible, Jack! (*To ALICE*)
We owe you an apology. Thank you for
saving our baby.

*ALICE smiles. JACK glares at her.*

*MAM enters through the gate, DAD from the house.*

MAM:    What on earth's going on here? I could hear
the racket halfway down the lane!

DAD:    Who's been worrying the pigs?

TOM:    It's nothing to fret about now, Mam. It's
over.

MAM:    Tom! Look at the state of you!

DAD:    Someone explain what's happened here!

JACK:    Nothing for you to worry about, Dad.
We're all fine. But Tom, you need to go
now. (*Gesturing to Alice*) And take *her* with
you!

ELLIE:    Please, Jack . . .

MAM:    Lower your voice, Jack. This is still my house
        and I can't abide shouting.

TOM:    Jack's right, we need to go. I'm sorry for the
        trouble, everyone. I think it's best if Alice and
        I go to the Spook's house. Then she can travel
        on to Staumin, to her family.

MAM:    Tom, Alice, before you go, you come inside
        and tell me what happened here . . . Things
        are getting darker, that's for sure.

TOM:    No, we'll go now, Mam. Things need to settle
        down, and I need to see Mr Gregory.

*TOM picks up the bag he brought down earlier. He and ALICE
turn to leave.*

*MAM turns to stare furiously at JACK.*

# SCENE ELEVEN
## THE SPOOK'S GARDEN

*THE SPOOK, TOM and ALICE sit underneath the tree.*

**TOM:** *Should* I have burned Mother Malkin?

**THE SPOOK:** As I told you, it's a cruel thing to burn a witch – I don't hold with it myself.

**TOM:** I suppose we will have to face Mother Malkin again, then.

**THE SPOOK:** No, lad. You can rest easy. She won't be coming back to this world. Not after what happened at the end. Remember what I told you about eating the heart of a witch? Well, those pigs of yours did it for us. Aye, you're safe from Mother Malkin. There are other threats out there just as bad, but you're safe for now. (*Teasing*) At least, until you make another silly mistake, eh?

**TOM:** Yes, Mr Gregory . . . I'm sorry.

**THE SPOOK:** Tom.

**TOM:** Yes?

**THE SPOOK** (*smiling*):
You did well . . . Right, lad, my belly is

rumbling. I'm going to get cleaned up for dinner. Don't be long, Tom. I want you to spend an hour in the library this evening. I can see you're tired, lad – but as you now know, there's no rest for the . . . well, a spook.

*THE SPOOK leaves, laughing to himself.*

ALICE:        l should be off now. I've got a long journey ahead.

TOM:        Why now? Stay another day.

ALICE:        If I stay around for much longer, I'll end up in your master's pit. It's not safe – Mr Gregory knows that. I'll stick to the original plan and head to my aunt in Staumin. She's a benign witch and a good woman. I'll be happy there.

TOM:        Look, Alice, I don't expect we will see each other again, but if you ever need help, try and get word to me. I'll miss you.

ALICE:        I'll miss you too. But we will meet again – ain't no doubt about that. Goodbye, Tom. Goodbye.

TOM:        Goodbye, Alice.

*ALICE exits, with TOM leaving in the opposite direction.*

*Blackout.*

# SUGGESTED
# CLASSROOM
# ACTIVITES

# ACT ONE

## SCENE ONE
## READING CHALLENGES

**True, False or Can't Tell**

*What is your opinion on these statements?*

1. Tom is thirteen years old.

2. Dad is tall.

3. Tom learned Greek at an early age.

4. If John Gregory takes on Tom as an apprentice, Tom will get paid twelve guineas.

5. Tom will become a spook.

6. Tom will be lonely working with John Gregory.

7. Tom is on a month's trial.

8. The Ward family have a cat.

9. Ellie left the room on her own.

10. Jack is cruel to Tom.

## Challenge the author

For one of your 'Can't Tell' answers argue whether
it is really true or false.

## Author's intent

1. How does the author show that Jack and Dad aren't
happy with John Gregory's attitude?

2. Is John Gregory a patient or impatient man? Say why.

3. Jack and Ellie are man and wife.
Would you say one of them is in charge? Why?

## Character empathy

*You need to give explanations for all your answers.*

1. Do you think Mam is loving towards Tom?

2. Is Jack worried about Tom leaving?

3. At the top of page 8, why is there an
awkward silence?

4. The characters below have had their emotions during the scene swapped. Join the right character to the right emotion during scene 1, explaining why you think this is so.

| Emotion | Character |
|---------|-----------|
| Cautious | Tom |
| Loving | Ellie |
| Worried | Dad |
| Proud | John Gregory |

5. Write a sentence that shows the way each of these characters feels about Tom.

**John Gregory**

**Mam**

**Ellie**

**Dad**

## WRITING CHALLENGE

Write a diary entry from Tom's point of view that shows his feelings about being sent to start his apprenticeship. Explain Tom's first impressions of the Spook, and his feelings about leaving his family. What is he looking forward to? And what is he going to miss?

## MEDIA CHALLENGE

Tom is about to leave with John Gregory to start his life as a spook's apprentice. However, you now have to prepare an idea for a spin-off series featuring one of the other characters.

Ellie is about to have a baby, Jack is now in charge of the farm, Dad is ageing and Mam doesn't seem to behave in quite the way you'd expect her to. Who would you choose for the spin off? What would the series be about and can you change the genre from children's fantasy horror?

# SCENES TWO & THREE

# READING CHALLENGES

**True, False or Can't Tell?**

*Can you decide whether each of these statements about Scene 3 are true or false – or can't you tell?*

1. After passing the test Tom would now make a good spook's apprentice.

2. John Gregory's dad was a cruel man.

3. John Gregory wasn't scared when he lived at 13 Watery Lane.

4. The miner was a jealous man.

5. John Gregory wanted Tom to be scared.

6. The ghast will leave the house eventually.

7. The miner meant to kill his wife.

8. Tom passed the test easily.

9. Tom was on time.

10. The fact that a spook notices evil presences and creatures is a good thing.

## Challenge the author

For one of your 'Can't Tell' answers argue whether it is really true or false.

## Author's Intent

1. How would you describe the atmosphere in Scene 2? Can you pick five words that create the atmosphere well?

2. How does the author create Tom's feelings in Scene 2?

3. What do you notice about Tom's dialogue compared to the Spook's in Scene 3?

4. Why do you think that John Gregory's dad isn't described by the Spook in detail in Scene 3?

5. In Scene 3, do Tom's actions or his words say more about how he is feeling? Why?

## Character Empathy

*All these questions are about Scene 3*

1. Can you write a short note from the miner's wife, reassuring her husband that she loves him, understands his frustrations and that she would never be unfaithful?

2. Write two notes from Tom to his mam. One should explain that he failed John Gregory's test and one that he has passed. Show his feelings in both.

3. What everyday activities and chores would make the miner feel frustrated whilst his wife was at work? Explain your choices.

4. Would the miner feel all of these emotions when trapped in the house? Explain why.

    a)      **jealousy**

    b)      **loneliness**

    c)      **anger**

    d)      **bitterness**

    e)      **hatred**

Explain your choices.

5. What could the wife have done differently
to make her husband feel better when he was
stuck at home and she was working?

6. Who do you think was more evil, the miner
who turned into the ghast or John Gregory's dad?
Explain your answer.

## Match the emotion

Match the feelings below to the characters they best suit
in Scene 3. Find a part of the script that shows this.

| | |
|---|---|
| Curious | John Gregory's dad |
| Vindictive and nasty | John Gregory |
| Regretful | Tom |

## WRITING CHALLENGE

Tom has sent a letter to his family in which he talks about
his worries. When Mam reads it, she senses that Tom may
run away from the Spook and come back home.
Can you write a letter to Tom from Mam persuading
him to stay, giving reasons.

## MEDIA CHALLENGE

In a dramatization of the story, which actor would you choose to play the Ghast? Talk about previous TV or films he has been in and why he would be ideal for the role.

# SCENES FOUR – SEVEN

# READING CHALLENGES

### True, False or Can't Tell

*What is your opinion on these statements about Scenes 4, 5, 6 and 7?*

1. Matty and Arthur were in the same class as Tom.

2. Lefty isn't a nickname.

3. Tom isn't generous because he refuses to give the boys food.

4. The boys are scared of Alice.

5. Alice wants to help Tom.

6. Alice isn't hungry.

7. Alice knows what happened to the last apprentice.

8. Tom is worried when he stares into Mother Malkin's pit.

9. Witches always wear pointy shoes.

10. John Gregory says that a witch's feet are pressed in to her shoes.

11. Tom is annoyed when the Spook says all women are trouble.

12. Tom is struggling to understand everything because he can't keep up with his note taking.

13. Tom doesn't realize what Alice is wearing.

14. The cakes need to be covered.

15. The Spook trusts Tom to be alone.

16. Tom respects his dad.

17. John Gregory is still away on spook's business.

18. Maisie is religious.

19. The village lads think that Tom has murdered the missing boy.

20. Mother Malkin drinks the blood of children.

21. The villagers have seen Mother Malkin.

22. The villagers laugh at Tom because he is an amusing person.

23. The villagers know where Mother Malkin is heading.

24. The villagers want to help Tom by making a plan.

## Challenge the author

For one of your 'Can't Tell' answers, argue whether it is really true or false.

## Author Intent

1. In Scene 5, Tom has a notebook. Why has the author given it an exact number of pages?

2. How does the author show us Tom's hesitancy in Scene 6?

3. What words and phrases are used in Scene 6 to show the danger of a witch?

4. Act 1 Scene 7 has more characters in it than any other scene, apart from the finale. Why do you think there are so many characters here?

5. What is the reason behind the stage direction on page 48, in Scene 7: *All the villagers laugh*?

6. The Seamstress is the only character in Scene 7 to show concern for Tom. How is it significant that she is female?

7. What is the author trying to show by indicating that none of the villagers volunteer to help Tom in Scene 7? Try to give two reasons for your answer.

## Character Empathy

*Give reasons for all your answers.*

1. In Scene 4, who is more threatening: Alice or the village boys?

2. Is Tom correct to keep hold of the sack in Scene 4 and not give any food to the boys?

3. Is Tom happy with the way his training has started in Scene 5?

4. In Scene 5, why doesn't the Spook give Tom more information before he instructs him to look down into Mother Malkin's pit?

5. In Scene 5 it could be argued that Tom shows a range of emotions towards the Spook. Pick three emotions Tom displays from this list:

**anger    respect    eagerness    fear    friendliness**

Give examples from the text to support your choices.

6. In Scene 6, we learn that the Spook has kept Mother Malkin in a pit for thirteen years. Do you judge him to be kind or nasty for this?

7. What advice do you think Tom's dad would have for him about giving Mother Malkin the bloodcakes?

8. What clues are there in Scenes 6 and 7 that Alice is under pressure, as well as Tom, to make sure that Mother Malkin gets the cakes?

9. In Scene 7 the Teacher says: *'I remember him. Never could trust him'*. What does this say about Tom's school life before he left?

10. After Mother Malkin escapes, the characters in Scene 7 have different emotions to Tom. Choose three from this list:

**Grocer and Baker**      **The village boys**

**Mother Malkin**         **Alice**

Give examples of their views and opinions from the text where you can.

## WRITING CHALLENGE

Write a 'How to Make Bloodcakes' instructional text. You will need to include the ingredients, the method, a warning and explain the consequences should the warning be ignored.

## MEDIA CHALLENGE

Imagine you are a director for the TV series of *The Spook's Apprentice*. What song and lyrics would you use to add power to the scene where Mother Malkin is in the pit, wanting to be free? Highlight the relevant lyrics that fit the narrative situation.

# ACT TWO

## SCENES ONE–FOUR

## READING CHALLENGES

### True, False or Can't Tell

*Can you decide whether each of these statements about Scenes 1, 2, 3 and 4 are true or false – or can't you tell?*

1. The messenger is poor.

2. John Gregory feels that the messenger is needlessly bothering him.

3. The messenger isn't literate and has poor reading skills.

4. Bony Lizzie has heard of Tom Ward.

5. Bony Lizzie isn't surprised that Tom defeated Mother Malkin.

6. Mother Malkin and Bony Lizzie don't like each other.

7. Alice feels guilty about helping take Tommy Brewer.

8. Alice is angry at Tom for rescuing Tommy.

9. Ellie has just had her baby.

10. Dad stays annoyed at Jack for his rudeness at Mam.

11. Dad knows that Tom is in trouble.

12. Baby Mary looks like Tom did as a baby.

13. The Ward family are a strong and close family.

14. Now that Jack is running the farm, he is the leader of the family.

15. Tom is still annoyed that Alice escaped.

16. Tom didn't have a pleasant smell.

17. Alice thought Tusk was going to capture Tom.

## Challenge the author

For one of your 'Can't Tell' answers argue whether it is really true or false.

## Author Intent

1. For casting the role, why is it an advantage not to have an age or detailed description for the Messenger who appears in Scene 1?

2. In Scene 1, why does the Messenger not knowing a lot about witches help the audience?

3. In Scene 3, Mam has meat burning in the kitchen whilst Mother Malkin's hideaway is on fire. What is the author trying to do here?

4. What clues does the author give us in Scene 3 that trouble is spreading across the County?

5. What hints does the author give us that Alice isn't evil in Scene 4?

6. Rewrite a line for Alice in Scene 4 that helps her give a hint to Tom about the trap?

## Character Empathy

1. In Scene 1, do you think the Spook is unnecessarily rude to the messenger?

2. In Scenes 1 and 2, what do the following characters feel about Mother Malkin escaping? The emotions are mixed up and not necessarily alongside the correct character name.

| | |
|---|---|
| **Alice** | **worry** |
| **Tom** | **panic** |
| **Bony Lizzie** | **relief** |
| **John Gregory** | **anger** |

3. Based on Alice's actions in the play so far,
what would you do to Alice if you were the Spook?

4. Who would you say shows most concern about
the fire in the village amongst Tom's family at the
beginning of Scene 3? Why is it significant that it
is this person?

5. The members of Tom's family have different
emotions after the fire in the village in Scene 3.
Match the character to the right emotion,
giving examples from the text where you can.

**Dad    Mam    Jack    Ellie**

**worried    unconcerned    unconcerned    worried**

6. What does the bickering between Bony Lizzie
and Mother Malkin in Scene 2 tell you about the
nature of witches, considering the fact that Makin
has been defeated?

7. In what way is Alice multi-layered?
Discuss all the different aspects to her character.

## WRITING CHALLENGE

In a poetic style (e.g. using rhyming couplets, alliteration,
repetition etc) write a short poem to be read aloud by
Mother Malkin chanting revenge on Tom.

## MEDIA CHALLENGE

Storyboard the battle between Tom and Mother Malkin, changing what you want.

## SCENES FIVE – SEVEN

## READING CHALLENGES

**True, False or Can't Tell**

*What is your opinion on these statements about Scenes 5, 6 and 7?*

1) Lizzie is going to kill Tom.

2) Bony Lizzie is in a rush to kill Tom because the Spook might turn up.

3) Bony Lizzie doesn't trust Alice.

4) Alice doesn't want to be part of the dark if she can avoid being so.

5) Alice doesn't know if she wants to be part of the Deane Clan.

6) The experience of facing Mother Malkin has made Tom less fearful.

7) Tom thinks he can defeat Bony Lizzie and Tusk.

8) The Spook was battling witches in Pendle.


9) The Spook knows Alice hadn't been practising blood or bone magic.

10) All witches in the county are evil.

11) The Spook decides to put Alice in a pit.

12) The Spook is annoyed at Alice.


## Challenge the author

For one of your 'Can't Tell' answers argue whether it is really true or false.


## Author intent

1) Why does the author have the characters run off in all different directions at the end of Scene 5?

2) In the novel of *The Spook's Apprentice* Tom and Alice escape Bony Lizzie and Tusk before John Gregory intervenes. Why does the play have the Spook find Alice and Tom with Bony Lizzie in Scene 6, instead of them going on the run?

3) In Scene 6, how does the author use punctuation to develop characterization?

4) In Scene 7 how does the author create the impression that John Gregory thinks Alice is sub-human?

5) How is Tom's warmness to Alice shown in Scene 7?

## Character Empathy

1) In Scene 5, the Midwife states, '*Poor boy must be exhausted after what he has been through, looking after things while you were off doing goodness knows what.*' She obviously blames the Spook for something. What for?

2) How does the Midwife's opinion fit into a theme of feminism in the play?

3) Tom is tricked twice by Alice. However he seems to lack bitterness, and even shows concern for her in Scene 6. Can you give two reasons why Tom behaves like this?

4) The Spook's first line to Lizzie in Scene 6 is, '*Hello, Lizzie.*' What does this tell you about the Spook's nature, and his relationship with Bony Lizzie?

5) By the end of Scene 7, which of the following emotions does John Gregory feel towards Alice and Tom?

anger    pride    relief    surprise

(Some of the emotions can be felt individually or jointly.)

6) Tom is mostly passive when John Gregory is inspecting Alice in Scene 7. What do you think Tom would say if he had the confidence to speak his mind?

## WRITING CHALLENGE

Write a persuasive piece either in favour of Alice going into a pit in John Gregory's garden or in favour of her being set free.

## MEDIA CHALLENGE

Write a newspaper article reporting the fact that John Gregory has defeated Bony Lizzie. Or construct a TV report that does the same thing.

# SCENES EIGHT – ELEVEN

## READING CHALLENGES

### True, False or Can't Tell

*Can you decide whether each of these statements about Scenes 8, 9, 10 and 11 are true or false – or can't you tell?*

1. In Scene 8, Tom thinks he is more important than Snout, and that is why he is rude to him.

2. Alice doesn't trust Snout.

3. Tom misses the birth of baby Mary.

4. Jack hates witches.

5. Jack wants Tom to stay and help at the farm.

6. Mother Malkin knows who Alice is.

7. Mother Malkin physically grabs hold of Alice.

8. Mother Malkin is going to kill Alice if she gets chance.

9. Jack is annoyed because Alice is contacting a witch through mirrors.

10. Jack is jealous of the way his dad treats Tom.

11. Jack has the power to make Tom and Alice leave.

12. Mother Malkin is somewhere in the farmhouse.

13. Ellie is confident that religion will help them.

14. Alice feels that she needs Tom.

15. Alice is still unsure whether she is part of
the dark or benign (good).

16. Ellie fainted because of Mother Malkin.

17. Mother Malkin was starved for thirteen years in
John Gregory's pit until the bloodcakes were given.

18. Jack has been possessed by Mother Malkin.

19. Alice feels she is partly to blame.

20. Tom needs Alice's help to defeat Snout.

21. Tom hits Snout.

22. Dad knew that the tinderbox he gave Tom
would be useful.

23. Tom doesn't have to kill Mother Malkin.

24. Tom would have burned Mother Malkin.

25. Mam knows the trouble isn't over.

26. Mother Malkin will never return.

27. The Spook feels that Tom has done well but could have done better.

28. Alice now feels safe around John Gregory.

29. Alice and Tom will meet in the future.


## Challenge the author

For one of your 'Can't Tell' answers argue whether it is really true or false.

## Author intent

1. What line in Scene 8 suggests that Snout may not be completely who he says he is?

2. In Scenes 8, 9 and 10, how is Ellie shown to be warmer than Jack to Tom?

3. What do you notice about Jack's behaviour when Mam is in the scene. Is it different to when she's not there?

4. In Scene 9, Alice is controlled through the mirror, how does this make the scene easy to stage? How does the breaking of the mirror act as a metaphor?

5. By Scene 10, what other genre has the play started to use?

6. Who does the author create as the stronger character, Alice or Tom? What are the reasons for your choice?

7. Throughout the play, gender is a key issue. How does the author use gender?

8. Why do you think the author has Alice leave at the end, when she could have stayed with Tom and the Spook?

9. In the novel of *The Spook's Apprentice*, the last action is with Tom and the Spook. However, the last dialogue in the play is between Alice and Tom. What do you think the reason for this is?

## Character empathy

1. Is Snout actually a humble person or is he pretending in his first conversation with Tom in Scene 8?

2. In Scene 8, what signs are there that Jack is getting annoyed at Tom being around?

3. Jack is annoyed at Tom for a number of reasons. Why is he annoyed on behalf of these people:

Dog    Mam    Mary    Ellie    Himself

Who of these is he most annoyed for?

4. At the beginning of Scene 9, do you think Alice is committed to leaving the dark?

5. Why is Jack annoyed that the mirror is broken in Scene 9?

6. What are the signs in Scene 9 that Jack is also jealous of Tom? What could he be jealous about?

7. How has Dad shown faith in Jack?

8. Choose a line from Scene 10 where it is clear that Alice has finally turned her back on the Dark.

9. Is Tom ready to be a spook, after the defeat of Mother Malkin?

10. We learn that Mother Malkin possessed Snout. Before this is confirmed, why would Tom be suspicious of the other characters below?

Ellie    Jack    Alice    Mam

11. How is Alice and Tom's relationship changed in the last scene when they suggest they might see each other again?

12. Does Tom need to apologize to the Spook when he returns to the house in Scene 11?

## WRITING CHALLENGE

Pick any part of the original novel of *The Spook's Apprentice*, link it to the play and discuss the differences.

## MEDIA CHALLENGE

Adding further stage direction, lighting notes and editing dialogue if you wish, cast a scene from the play and perform it with your fellow actors.

# NOTES

# NOTES

# NOTES

# NOTES

**Now you've studied the play you might like to read the original novel. Keep reading for the opening . . .**

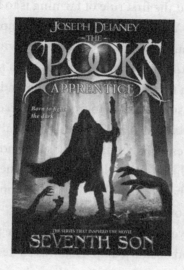

When the Spook arrived, the light was already beginning to fail. It had been a long, hard day and I was ready for my supper.

'You're sure he's a seventh son?' he asked. He was looking down at me and shaking his head doubtfully.

Dad nodded.

'And you were a seventh son too?'

Dad nodded again and started stamping his feet impatiently, splattering my breeches with droplets of brown mud and manure. The rain was dripping from the peak of his cap. It had been raining for most of the month. There were new leaves on the trees but the spring weather was a long time coming.

My dad was a farmer and his father had been a farmer too, and the first rule of farming is to keep the farm together. You can't just divide it up amongst your children; it would get smaller and smaller with each generation until there was nothing left. So a father leaves his farm to his eldest son. Then he finds jobs for the rest. If possible, he tries to find each a trade.

He needs lots of favours for that. The local blacksmith is one option, especially if the farm is big and he's given the blacksmith plenty of work. Then it's odds on that the blacksmith will offer an apprenticeship, but that's still only one son sorted out.

I was his seventh, and by the time it came to me all the favours had been used up. Dad was so desperate that he was trying to get the Spook to take me on as his apprentice. Or at least that's what I thought at the time. I should have guessed that Mam was behind it.

She was behind a lot of things. Long before I was born, it was her money that had bought our farm. How else could a seventh son have afforded it? And Mam wasn't County. She came from a land far across the sea.

Most people couldn't tell, but sometimes, if you listened very carefully, there was a slight difference in